YEAR 3

NAPLAN*-style NUMERACY

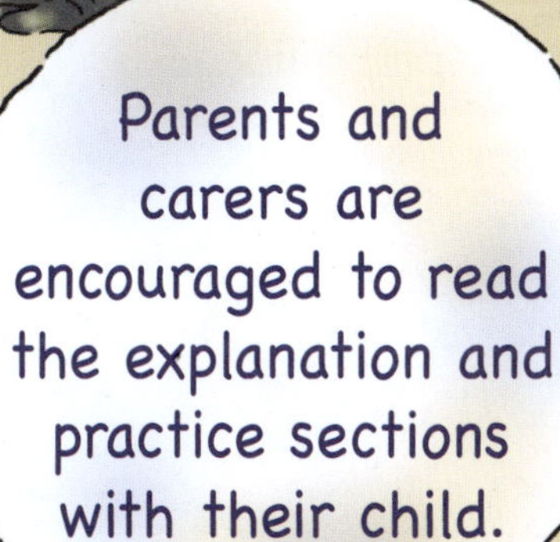

Annie Hughes
Olwen Narbey

Illustrated by
Janice Bowles

*This is not an officially endorsed publication of the NAPLAN program and is produced by Pascal Press independently of Australian Governments.

About this book

This book is designed to review the skills required for the Numeracy component of the Year 3 NAPLAN test and to practise NAPLAN*-style questions.

The book commences with four **Pre-tests,** to help identify any areas of weakness that may require special attention.
The Pre-tests are followed by **20 units** that cover the key maths topics Year 3 students need to understand so that they can approach their NAPLAN Numeracy test with confidence.

Each unit begins with a brief explanation of the maths concept or strategy and gives you and your child the information you need to work through the questions successfully.

We practise: provides worked examples for you and your child to discuss together, paying particular attention to the thinking processes required to understand the concept or strategy.

You practise: gives your child the opportunity to practise the concept or strategy independently.

Problem solving: at the end of each topic there are NAPLAN-style problem-solving questions for your child to practise.

16 page pull-out test: the Sample NAPLAN test at the back of the book should be attempted once the bulk of the book has been completed and you feel that your child has a good grasp of the key concepts in the book.

All answers for each of the units and tests are at the back of the book.

As parents we hope you find this a helpful guide.

All the best!

Annie and Ollie

*This is not an officially endorsed publication of the NAPLAN program and is produced by Pascal Press independently of Australian Governments.

Contents & Checklist

Number & Algebra (Units 1–10)

Measurement & Geometry (Units 11–18)

Statistics & Probability (Units 19–20)

*This is not an officially endorsed publication of the NAPLAN program and is produced by Pascal Press independently of Australian Governments.

INTRODUCTION to NAPLAN*

The National Assessment Program for Literacy and Numeracy (NAPLAN) is a Federal Government initiative that requires the assessment of skills in literacy and numeracy across all Australian schools for students in years 3, 5, 7 and 9. It was introduced in 2008 to replace the previous state-based assessment programs.

NAPLAN is held annually in May. All students receive an individualised report on their performance, which can be compared to the average performance of all students in Australia. The report contains a description of each assessment area and identifies the skills being assessed.

Using this book to prepare for the NAPLAN test

The NAPLAN Numeracy test covers all three major strands of the Mathematics curriculum:

- Number and Algebra
- Measurement and Geometry
- Statistics and Probability.

Questions vary between multiple-choice, where students are required to identify the correct answer to a question by shading the correct bubble, or short answer. The units in this book cover the three strands of the Mathematics curriculum and are based on previous NAPLAN tests.

Pre-test

Four Pre-tests have been included on pages 6–9 to help you identify your child's areas of weakness. Once completed, use the marking grid on page 10 to guide you to the units that will be most helpful. Answers are supplied on page 11.

Problem solving

The NAPLAN Numeracy test includes many questions written in the form of a problem. This style of question has been included at the end of each unit to provide your child with ample practice with this approach.

Pull-out test

The back of the book has a 16 page, pull-out Sample NAPLAN test. This will give your child a good idea of what to expect during the actual exam. The results will provide the information you need to pinpoint areas that require attention. We recommend that your child take this test under timed conditions, when the bulk of the book has been successfully completed.

*This is not an officially endorsed publication of the NAPLAN program and is produced by Pascal Press independently of Australian Governments.

HINTS and TIPS

Exam equipment:

* Make sure you have at least TWO sharp HB or 2B pencils — in case one breaks.
* Make sure you have an eraser — in case you mark the wrong bubble by mistake.

Reading time:

* Read all the instructions carefully.
* Read each question TWICE so you understand exactly what is being asked.

Timing:

* You will have 45 minutes to do the NAPLAN paper, which will have about 35 questions. This means you will have just over a minute per answer.
* Work steadily through the questions, without rushing or dawdling. Don't be put off by an answer that seems too obvious or too simple.
* Start at Question 1 and work through the questions in order. If you jump around too much, you risk accidentally missing a question.
* Skip any questions that you can't do, rather than spending a long time on them. You might run out of time to do the easier questions!
* After you have worked through all the questions, return to any that you skipped earlier and have another go at answering them.

Answering multiple-choice questions:

* First, try to answer the question without looking at the choices. Once you think you know the correct answer, read through the choices.
* Fill in the answer bubble properly

  like this  ✓

  NOT like this  ✗

Review:

* Go back and check your answers if you have time at the end.
* Don't change an answer unless you are sure it is wrong!

Tricky questions:

* Look carefully at the answers. Are there any that you know are wrong? Change them!
* If you can't answer a difficult question — guess!

PRE-TEST 1

1. 8 × 5 = ____

2. Convert 3500 millilitres into litres.

____

Use this graph to complete the following questions.

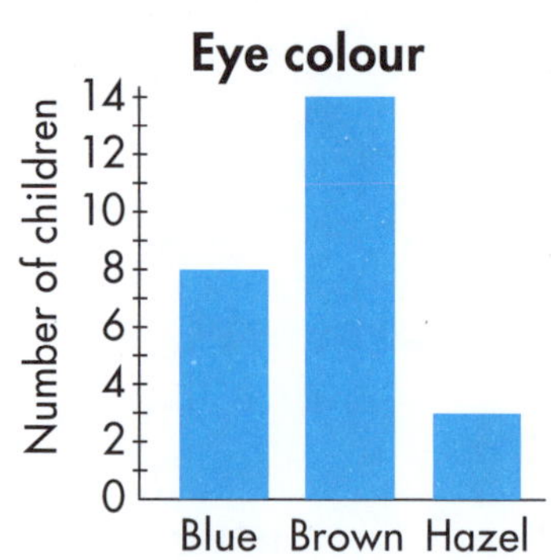

3. Draw the tally marks. Write the total.

Eye colour	Tally	Total
Blue		
Brown		
Hazel		

4. How many more children have blue eyes than hazel eyes? ____

5. Altogether, how many children were surveyed? ____

Answer these questions.

6. What is the chance of rolling 1 on a dice? Circle your answer.

Unlikely **Almost certain**

7. How much does this bag of potatoes weigh?

____ kg

8. What is the time?

____ minutes to ____

9. Without looking, Femi takes a pencil out of his pencil case. What colour is it most likely to be?

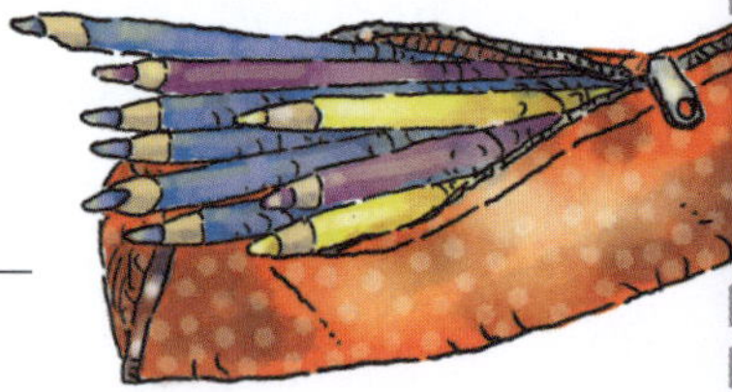

____

10. 27 ÷ 3 = ____

11. Show the digital time on the clock.

9:25

12. How long is this cricket bat?

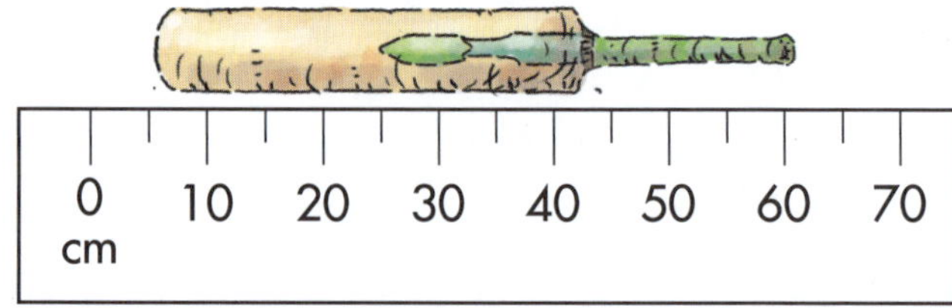

____ cm

13. 3 × 12 = ____

14. What is the chance of the spinner's arrow stopping on blue? Circle your answer.

Unlikely

Almost certain

15. Show the matching digital time.

12 minutes to 5

__ __ : __ __

PRE-TEST 2

1. 50 000 + 2000 + 400 + 3

= ____________

2. 46 + 38 = ______

Use the grid to complete the following questions.

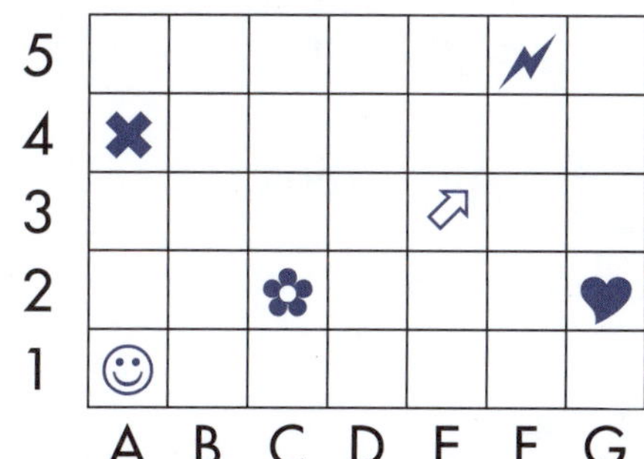

3. Mark a triangle on the grid at D5.

4. Draw the shape at coordinates G2.

5. If you move the lightning bolt 4 squares to the left, what are its new coordinates? ______

Answer these questions.

6. 55 – 26 = ______

7. How many days in a fortnight? ______

8. Continue the number sequence.

95, 90, 85, ______, ______, ______

9. Expand this number: 21 869

20 000 + ________________________

10. What is the date of the third Saturday?

December						
S	M	T	W	T	F	S
				1	2	3
4	5	6	7	8	9	10
11	12	13	14	15	16	17
18	19	20	21	22	23	24
25	26	27	28	29	30	31

____

11. What is the rule for the following number sequence?

1, 5, 9, 13, 17, 21

Rule: ____________

12. 173 – 15 = ______

13. 4285 + ______ = 4785

14. Milly got to the train station at 10:00 am.

Roma Street Train Station				
Departure times				
9:30	9:50	10:10	10:30	10:50

What time is the next train leaving?

____

15. Draw the next shape in the pattern.

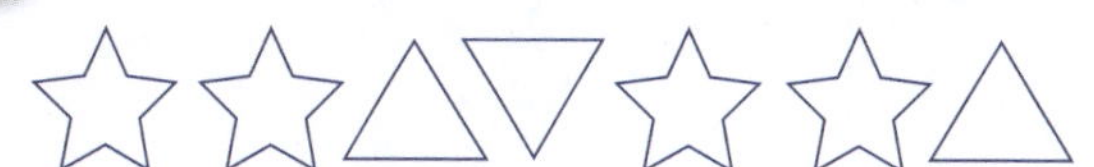

PRE-TEST 3

1 Circle the picture that is not symmetrical.

2 Draw this object rotated a three-quarter turn clockwise.

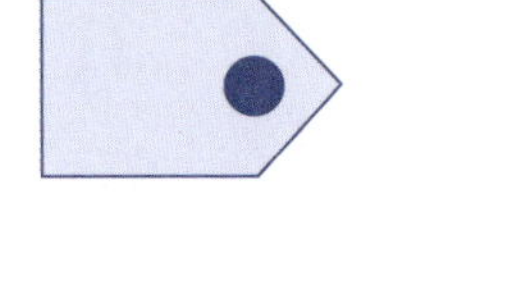

3
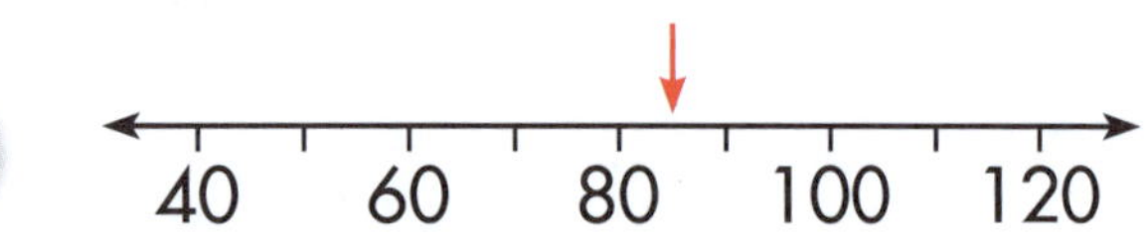

What is the arrow pointing to? ______

4 True or false? 98 > 100 __________

5 What is the arrow pointing to?

______

6 $10.00 – $6.15 = _________

7 Draw the lines of symmetry on the shape.

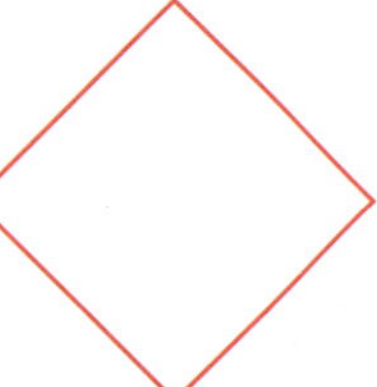

Use the grid to complete the following questions.

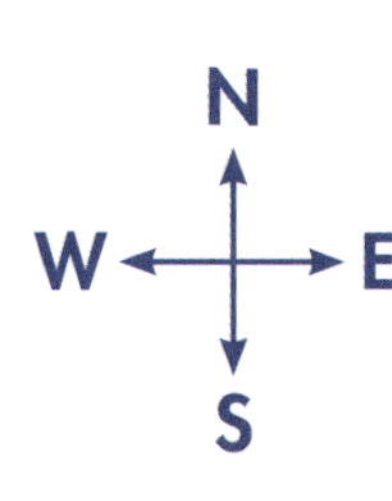

8 What compass direction does the dog have to move along to get to his bowl of food? ________

9 Start at the teddy bear.
Move 2 squares North.
Turn 90° anticlockwise
and move ahead 1 square.
What animal do you land on? ______

Answer these questions.

10 100 more than 602 is ______.

11 How much juice is in the jug?

______

12 $5.00 – $1.85 = ________

13 Ruby folds a square piece of paper in half and cuts out some shapes. What will it look like when she unfolds it? Shade the bubble of your answer.

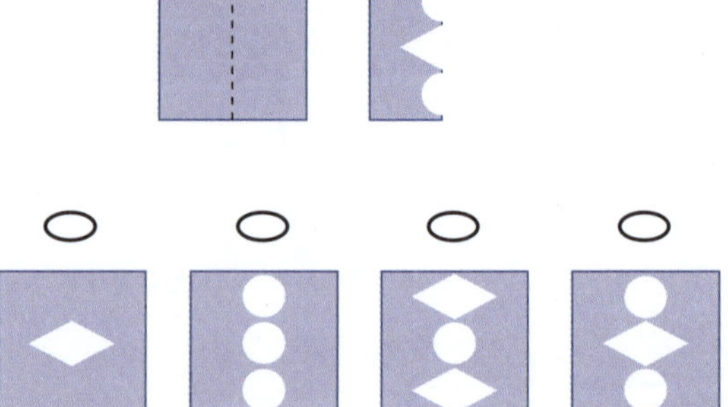

14 What position comes after 6th? ______

15 How much change will I get if I pay $5.00 for glue that costs $2.30?

____

PRE-TEST 4

1. How many faces does a cylinder have? ____

2. What is the name of this shape?

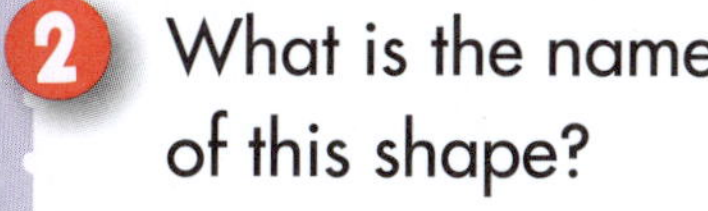

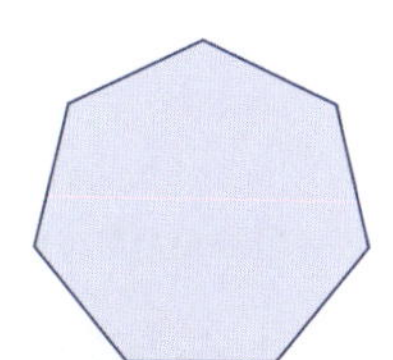

____

3. Write the shaded fraction.

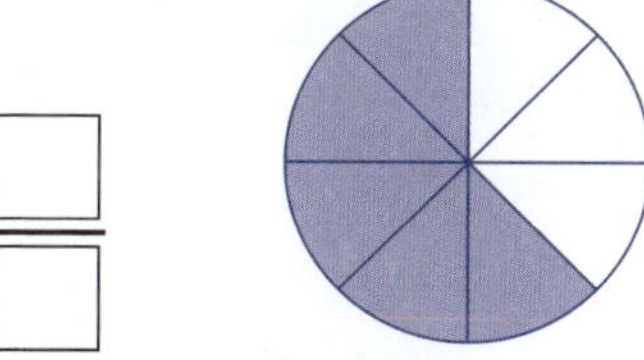

$\frac{\square}{\square}$

4. How much money is this?

____

5. Six eighths is equivalent to how many quarters?

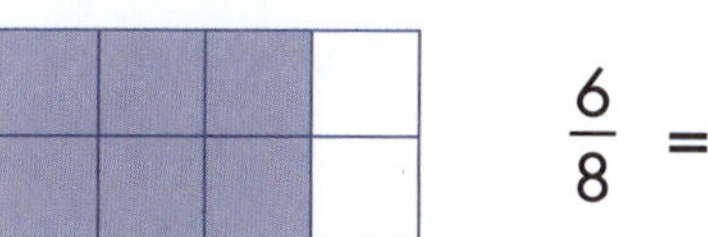

$\frac{6}{8} = \frac{\square}{\square}$

6. What is the name of this 3D object?

____

7. Write the fraction that is shaded.

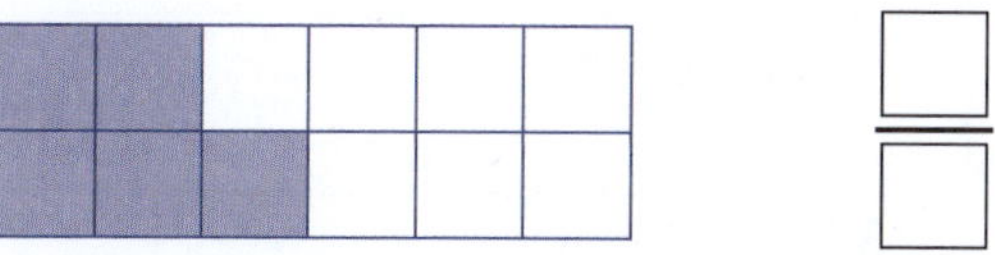

$\frac{\square}{\square}$

8. Circle the hexagon.

 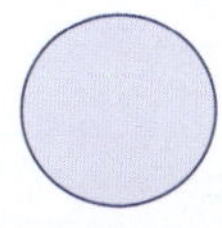 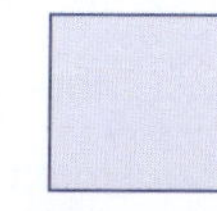 

9. What is the equivalent fraction?

$\frac{1}{2} = \frac{2}{4} = \frac{\square}{8}$

10. What 3D object would this net make?

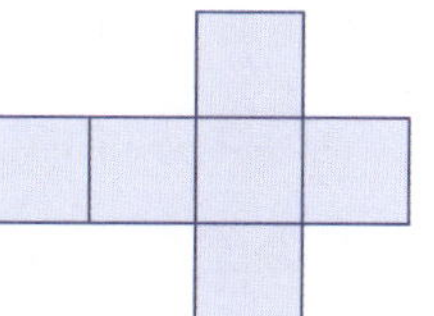

____

11. Write the fraction of ladybugs that are green.

$\frac{\square}{\square}$

12. Draw the missing coin to make the total $1.85.

13. Circle the group of money that totals $3.40.

14. How many sides does a nonagon have? ____

15. One third is equivalent to how many sixths?

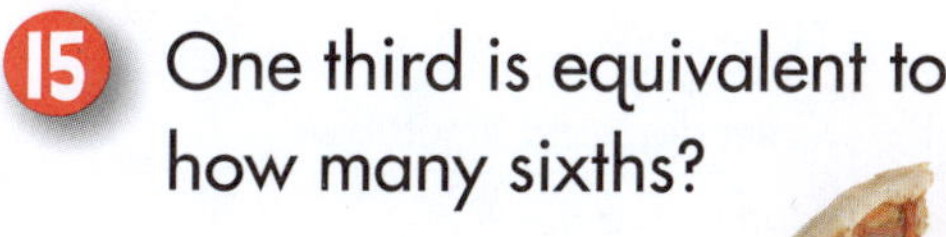

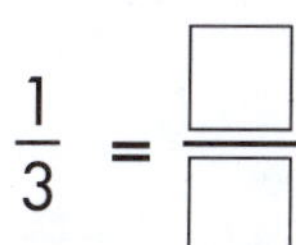

$\frac{1}{3} = \frac{\square}{\square}$

PRE-TEST MARKING GUIDE

Complete the marking guide below to assess your child's understanding of important mathematical concepts. Use the guide to help you to identify the key areas and to consolidate essential skills.

Step 1: Your child completes a test.

Step 2: Mark the test.

Step 3: Find the question number and record your child's result in the answer box.

Step 4: Decide on the topics you want to focus on with your child.

Pre-test 1			
Question	**Unit**	**Topic**	**✓ or ✗**
1	2	Multiplication and division	
2	11	Length, mass and capacity	
3	20	Graphs and data	
4	20	Graphs and data	
5	20	Graphs and data	
6	19	Chance	
7	11	Length, mass and capacity	
8	12	Telling the time	
9	19	Chance	
10	2	Multiplication and division	
11	12	Telling the time	
12	11	Length, mass and capacity	
13	2	Multiplication and division	
14	19	Chance	
15	12	Telling the time	
Pre-test 2			
1	3	Place value	
2	1	Addition and subtraction	
3	14	Coordinates	
4	14	Coordinates	
5	14	Coordinates	
6	1	Addition and subtraction	
7	13	Calendars and timetables	
8	4	Number patterns	
9	3	Place value	
10	13	Calendars and timetables	
11	4	Number patterns	
12	1	Addition and subtraction	
13	3	Place value	
14	13	Calendars and timetables	
15	4	Number patterns	

Pre-test 3			
Question	**Unit**	**Topic**	**✓ or ✗**
1	16	Symmetry	
2	16	Symmetry	
3	5	Number lines	
4	6	Ordering numbers	
5	5	Number lines	
6	10	Money – change	
7	16	Symmetry	
8	15	Position	
9	15	Position	
10	6	Ordering numbers	
11	5	Number lines	
12	10	Money – change	
13	16	Symmetry	
14	6	Ordering numbers	
15	10	Money – change	
Pre-test 4			
1	18	3D objects	
2	17	2D shapes	
3	7	Fractions	
4	9	Adding money	
5	8	Equivalent fractions	
6	18	3D objects	
7	7	Fractions	
8	17	2D shapes	
9	8	Equivalent fractions	
10	18	3D objects	
11	7	Fractions	
12	9	Adding money	
13	9	Adding money	
14	17	2D shapes	
15	8	Equivalent fractions	

PRE-TEST ANSWERS

Pre-test 1

1 40

2 3.5 L or 3 L 500 mL

3

Eye colour	Tally	Total
Blue	~~||||~~ |||	8
Brown	~~||||~~ ~~||||~~ ||||	14
Hazel	|||	3

4 5

5 25

6 Unlikely

7 2.5 kg or 2 kg 500 g

8 8 minutes to 3

9 Blue

10 9

11 

12 55 cm

13 36

14 Unlikely

15 4:48

Pre-test 2

1 52 403

2 84

3 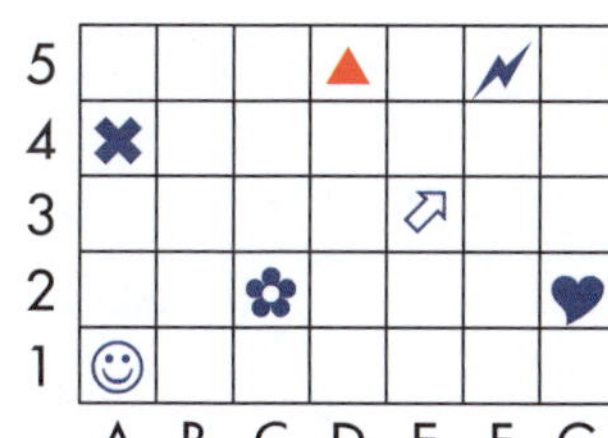

4 ♥

5 B5

6 29

7 14

8 80, 75, 70

9 20 000 + 1000 + 800 + 60 + 9

10 17th December

11 Rule: Add 4

12 158

13 500

14 10:10

15 

Pre-test 3

1 

2

3 85

4 False

5 40 g

6 $3.85

7 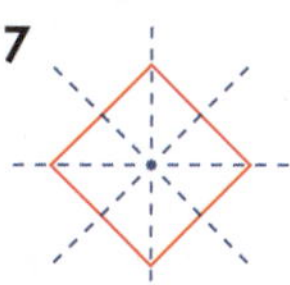

8 East

9 Cat

10 702

11 $\frac{3}{4}$ L, 0.75 L or 750 mL

12 $3.15

13 

14 7th

15 $2.70

Pre-test 4

1 3 faces

2 Heptagon

3 $\frac{5}{8}$

4 $5.75

5 $\frac{3}{4}$

6 Triangular prism

7 $\frac{5}{12}$

8

9 $\frac{4}{8}$

10 Cube

11 $\frac{5}{8}$ of the ladybugs are green

12 

13 

14 9

15 $\frac{2}{6}$

ADDITION and SUBTRACTION STRATEGIES

NUMBER & ALGEBRA

Addition and subtraction jump strategies can help you work out number problems.

Start with the bigger number.

Split the other number into parts. Splitting a number is called **partitioning**.

3 To **add** a number, **jump forwards** along the number line to find the sum.

16 + 32 = ?

Start with the bigger number: 32

Split the other number: 16 = 10 and 6

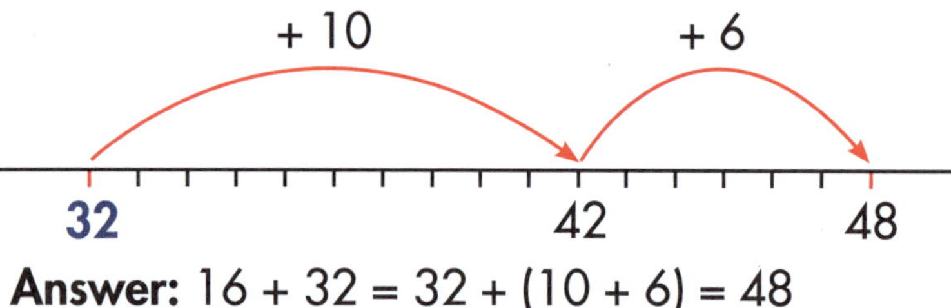

Answer: 16 + 32 = 32 + (10 + 6) = 48

To **subtract** a number, **jump backwards** along the number line to find the difference.

48 – 16 = ?

Start with the bigger number: 48

Split the other number: 16 = 10 and 6

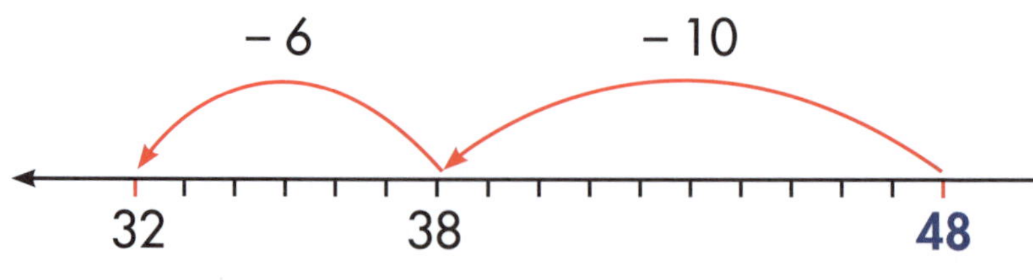

Answer: 48 – 16 = 48 – 10 – 6 = 32

Rainbow facts help you quickly split numbers. Remember these number pairs!

We practise

Use the addition jump strategy to find the sum.

15 + 74 = 74 + (10 + 5) = 89

Use the subtraction jump strategy to find the difference.

35 – 12 = 35 – 10 – 2 = 23

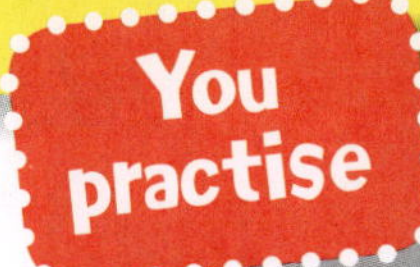

Use the addition jump strategy to find the sum.

1. 37 + 11 = ________ 37
2. 34 + 16 = ________ 34
3. 71 + 25 = ________
4. 145 + 13 = ________

Use the subtraction jump strategy to find the difference.

5. 66 – 14 = ________ 66
6. 35 – 15 = ________ 35
7. 96 – 21 = ________
8. 128 – 11 = ________

Problem solving

9. Mary is giving a bookmark to each of the 24 children in her class. She has 46 bookmarks. How many will she have left?

____

BOB time!

10. Josh got $6 for cleaning his room, $22 for mowing the lawns and $8 for washing the car. How much pocket money did Josh earn?

____

UNIT 2 MULTIPLICATION and DIVISION STRATEGIES

Multiplication

Use dots in rows and columns to make an **array**.

3 × 9 (3 rows of 9) = ?

3 × 9 = 27

Jump forwards on a ruler or **number line**. Count how many times you jump.

4 × 5 (4 groups of 5) = ?

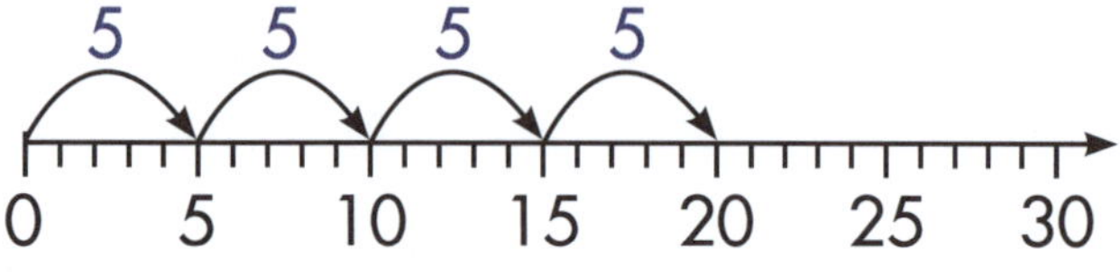

4 × 5 = 20

Use **repeated addition** by adding the number to itself.

5 × 7 = ?

5 + 5 + 5 + 5 + 5 + 5 + 5 = 35

Division

Use **grouping** to repeat a subtraction.

18 ÷ 3 = ?

How many groups of 3 are in 18?

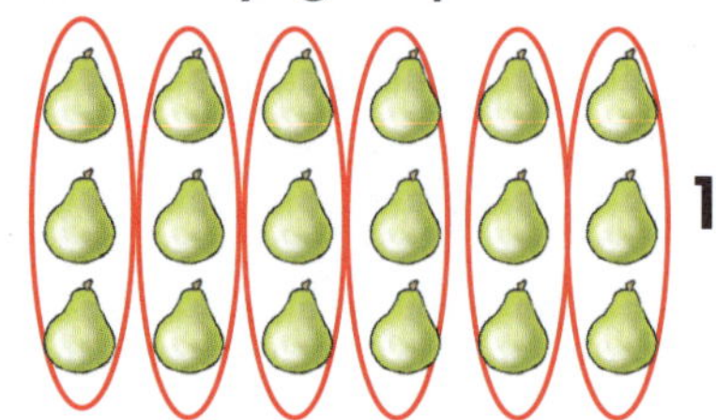

18 ÷ 3 = 6

Start at the number being divided and **jump backwards** along a ruler or number line. Count how many times you jump.

24 ÷ 6 = ?

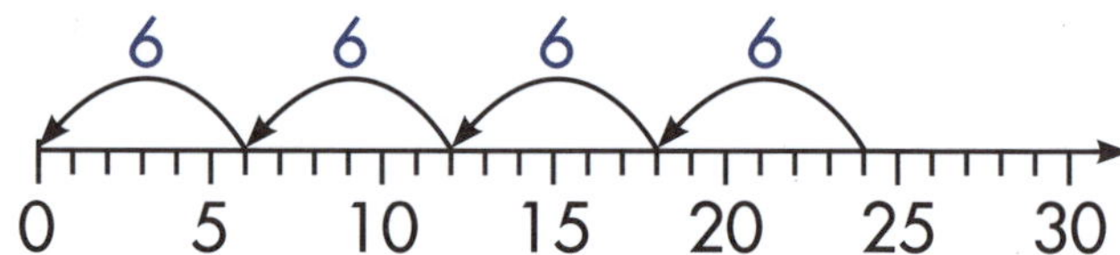

4 groups back

24 ÷ 6 = 4

Multiplication and division are opposites. You can rewrite a problem like this:

18 ÷ 2 = 9
2 × 9 = 18

We practise

Use an array to show 2 × 3.

2 × 3 = 6

Use the number line to show 3 × 9 = 27.

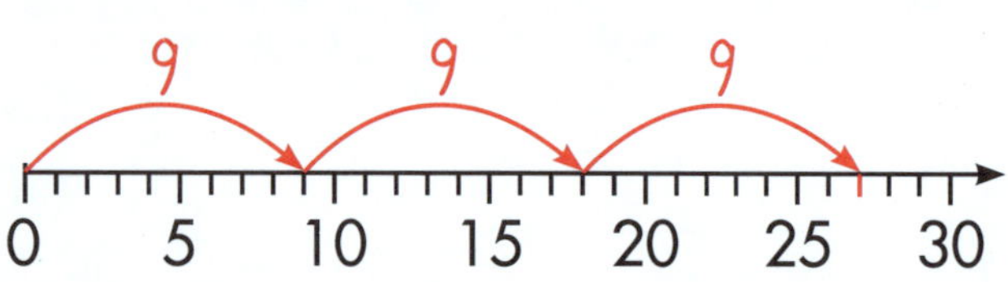

Use grouping to show 12 ÷ 2.

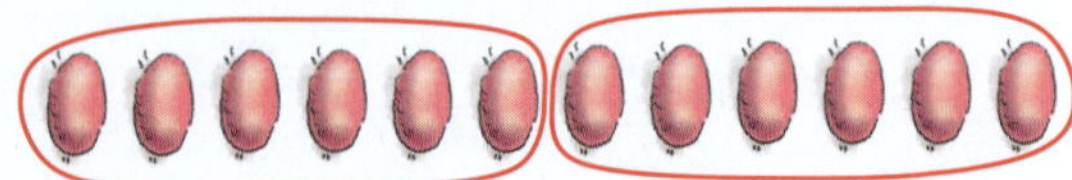

12 ÷ 2 = 6

Use the number line to show 16 ÷ 4 = 4.

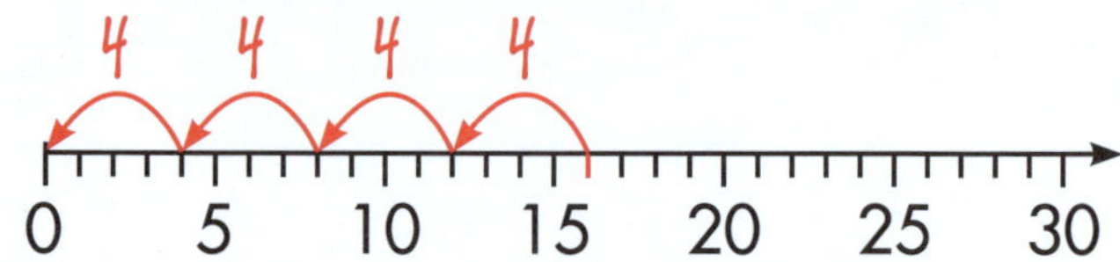

Remember, rows go across!

Describe the arrays and write the multiplication.

1 

____ rows of ____

____ × ____ = ____

2 

____ rows of ____

____ × ____ = ____

3

____ rows of ____

____ × ____ = ____

Use the arrays above to help you solve these division problems.

4 _____ ÷ 4 = 4

5 _____ ÷ 2 = 3

6 _____ ÷ 5 = 3

Use the number line to work out the multiplication and division problems.

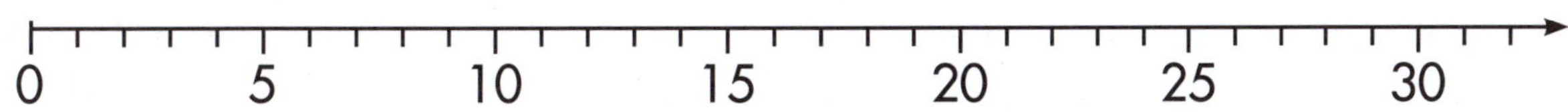

7 3 × 10 = _____

8 5 × 5 = _____

9 7 × 4 = _____

10 24 ÷ 3 = _____

11 16 ÷ 4 = _____

12 10 ÷ 5 = _____

Rewrite these sums as multiplication problems, then work out the answers.

13 6 + 6 + 6 + 6

____

14 12 + 12 + 12

____

15 8 + 8 + 8 + 8 + 8

____

Problem solving

16 Grandma made 16 biscuits. She baked them all on one tray. How many rows of 8 biscuits were on the tray?

____

17 Grandma has four grandchildren, who shared the biscuits equally. How many biscuits did each grandchild receive?

____

BOB time!

PLACE VALUE

Every number is made up of digits with different place values.
Place value tells you how much each digit is worth.
You can use a chart to help you work out place values.

	Ten thousands (10 000)	Thousands (1000)	Hundreds (100)	Tens (10)	Ones/ units (1)
68 451	6	8	4	5	1

The 8 in this number is worth 8 × **1000** = 8000.

The 5 in this number is worth 5 × **10** = 50.

10 000 = 10 thousands = 100 hundreds = 1000 tens = 10 000 ones

4658
Face value: the digit itself = 5
Place value: the column it is in = tens
Total value: face × place 5 × 10 = 50

Partitioning means to separate a number into parts. **Expanding** means to show the value of each digit in a number. We can **partition** or **expand** numbers when we know about place value.

4 ten thousands, 5 thousands, 6 hundreds, 2 tens, 1 one or 1 unit

45 621 = 40 000 + 5000 + 600 + 20 + 1
= Forty-five thousand, six hundred and twenty-one

Complete the place value chart.

	Ten thousands (10 000)	Thousands (1000)	Hundreds (100)	Tens (10)	Ones/ units (1)
83 985	8	3	9	8	5

Expand this number.

83 985 = 80 000 + 3000 + 900 + 80 + 5

Write this number in words.

83 985 = Eighty-three thousand, nine hundred and eighty-five

We practise

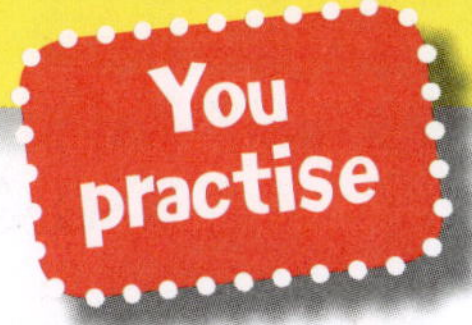

Complete the place value chart.

	Ten thousands (10 000)	Thousands (1000)	Hundreds (100)	Tens (10)	Ones/ units (1)
1 437					
2 5821					
3 85 348					
4 14					

Write the place value of the red digit.
Choose from: Ten thousands, Thousands, Tens, Ones.

5 1790 ____________________

6 18 506 ____________________

7 582 ____________________

8 92 548 ____________________

Expand these numbers.

9 386 = ____________________

10 97 105 = ____________________

11 4583 = ____________________

12 21 520 = ____________________

Write these numbers in words.

13 45 600 ____________________

14 792 ____________________

Problem solving

15 Look at the two calculator displays below. What did Tom have to do to change the first display into the second display in just one move?

5731
5431

- ○ Add 300
- ○ Take away 3
- ○ Add 3
- ○ Take away 300

NUMBER PATTERNS

The key to all **number sequences** and **patterns** is to **identify the rule**.

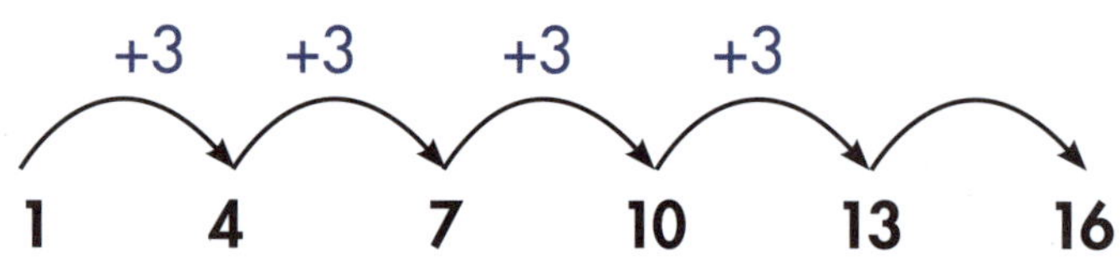

1 4 7 10 13 16

1. **Up or down:** Are the numbers getting larger (adding) or smaller (taking away)?
   Adding
2. **Difference:** Find the difference between two numbers.
   3
3. **Identify the rule:** How do you get from one number to the next number?
   Add 3
4. **Apply:** Use the rule to find the missing or next numbers in the sequence.

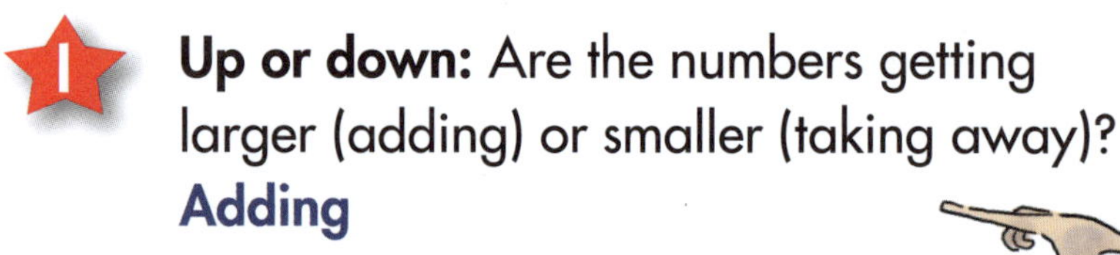

Try jumping along a ruler to find the rule.

Check at least 4 numbers, shapes or objects to identify the rule.

We practise

Write the next three numbers in the sequence, then write the rule.

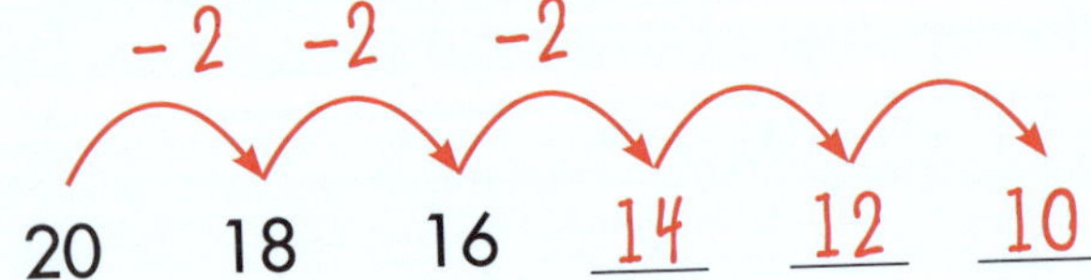

20 18 16 14 12 10 Rule: - 2

Complete the pattern, then write the rule.

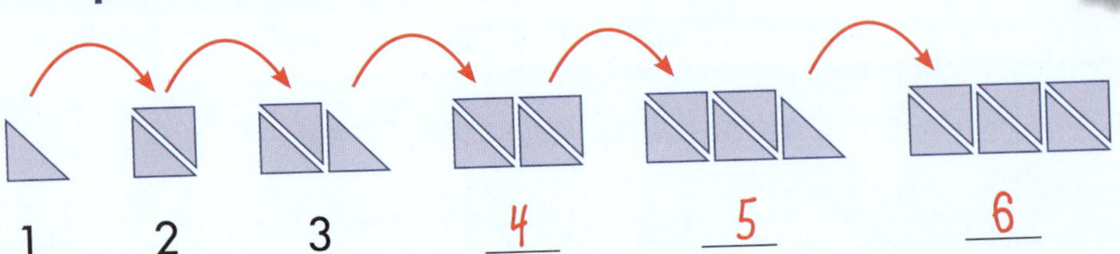

1 2 3 4 5 6

Rule: + 1 triangle

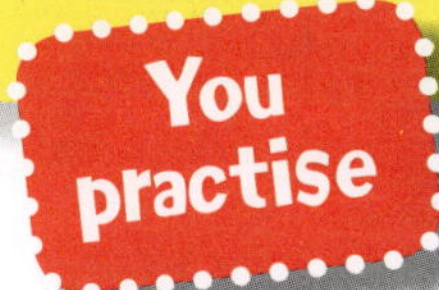

Identify the rule, then fill in the missing numbers.

1. 5 10 15 _____ _____ _____ Rule: [ ]
2. 23 25 27 _____ _____ _____ Rule: [ ]
3. 80 70 60 _____ _____ _____ Rule: [ ]
4. 1006 _____ 1010 _____ 1014 _____ Rule: [ ]

Draw the next three shapes in the patterns.

5.
6.

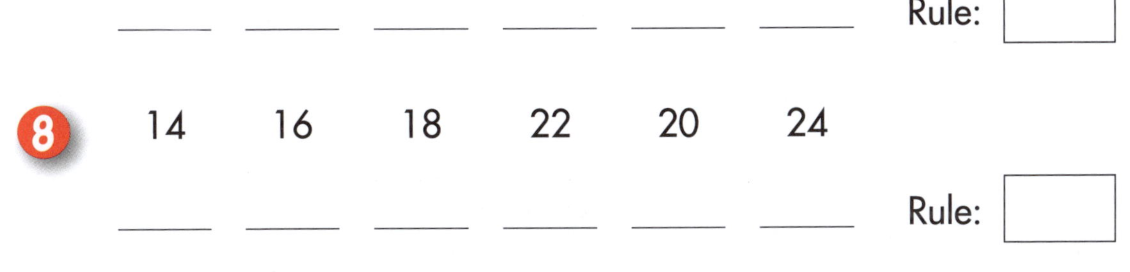

Two numbers in each sequence have been swapped around. Identify the rules, then write the sequences in the correct orders.

7. 20 30 50 40 60 70

_____ _____ _____ _____ _____ _____ Rule: [ ]

8. 14 16 18 22 20 24

_____ _____ _____ _____ _____ _____ Rule: [ ]

Problem solving

9. What are the first three numbers in this sequence?

_____ _____ _____ 12 15 18 21 24

- ○ 4, 7, 10
- ○ 11, 10, 9
- ○ 3, 6, 9
- ○ 2, 6, 10

BOB time!

NUMBER LINES

Number lines help us **order** numbers. We see number lines in many places: in Maths books, but also on rulers, measuring jugs, scales and clocks.

Follow the steps to find out what number the **green** arrow is pointing to.

An **interval** is the space between marks.

1. First work out the size of one interval.
3. Divide one interval into smaller equal parts. For example, 2, 4 or 5 parts.

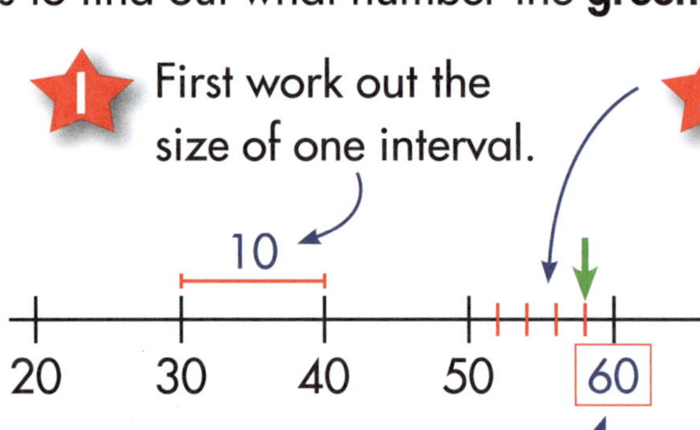

2. Fill in the missing numbers.
4. Count to work out what number the arrow is pointing to.

Answer: The arrow is pointing to 58.

Here are some commonly used intervals.

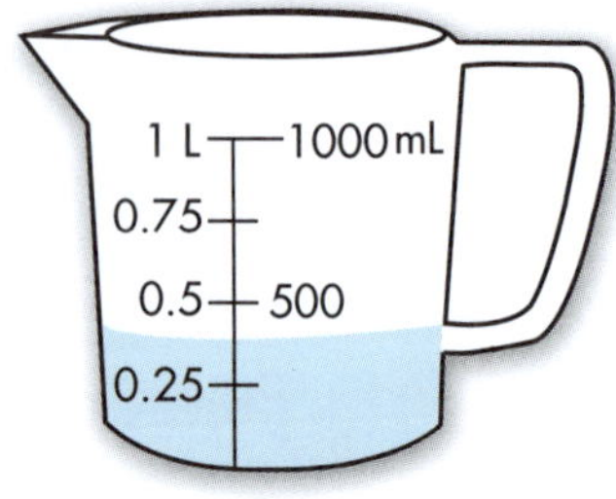

We practise

What number is the arrow pointing to?

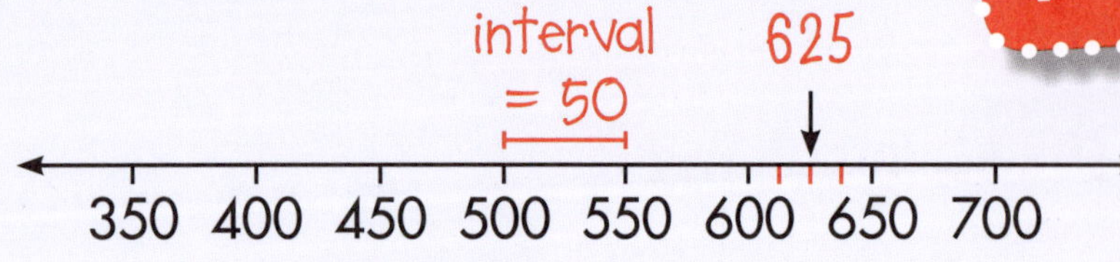

Draw an arrow at 3.5 mL.

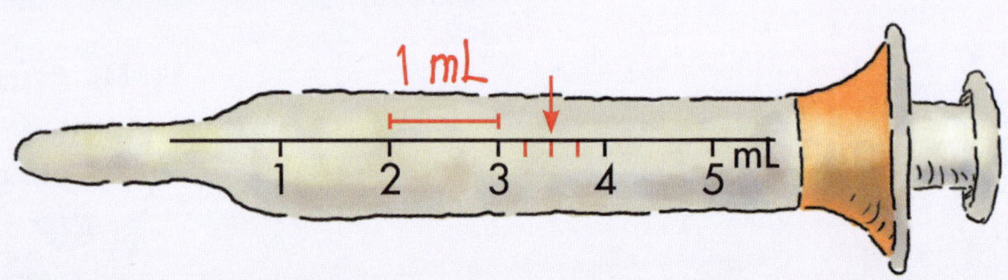

To find the interval, see if there are jumps of 1s, 2s, 5s, 10s, 20s or 50s.

Fill in the missing numbers, then identify where the arrows are pointing.

1 Arrow = ______

60 61 ☐ ☐ 64 65 66 67 68 ☐ 70

2 Arrow = ______

400 410 ☐ 430 440 450 460 470 ☐ 490 500

Use intervals to answer these questions.

3 How much juice is in the jug?

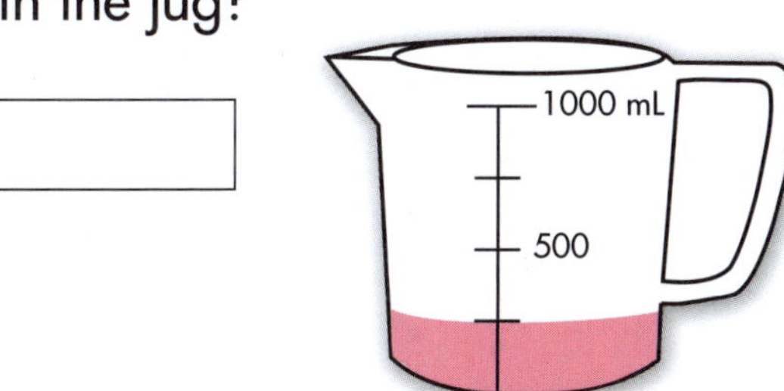

4 How heavy is the orange?

5 How long is the toy car?

6 How much water is in the bucket?

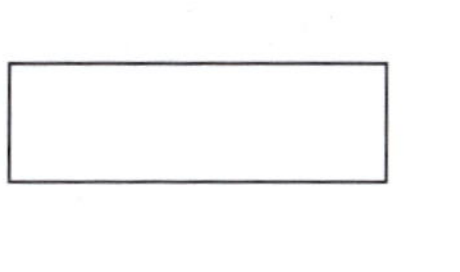

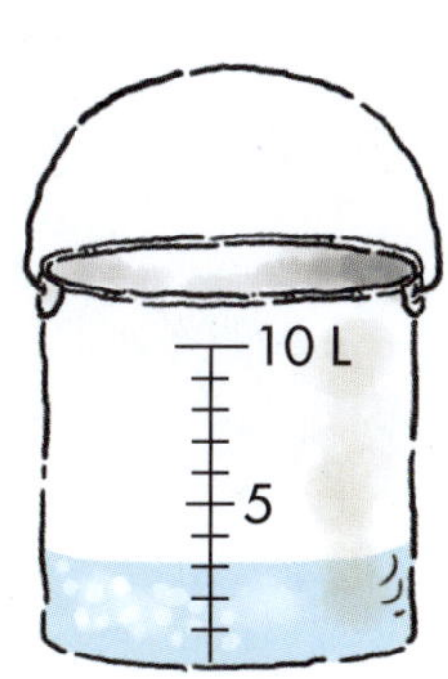

Draw arrows to mark the numbers on the number lines.

Hint: First divide the intervals into smaller equal parts.

7 **120**

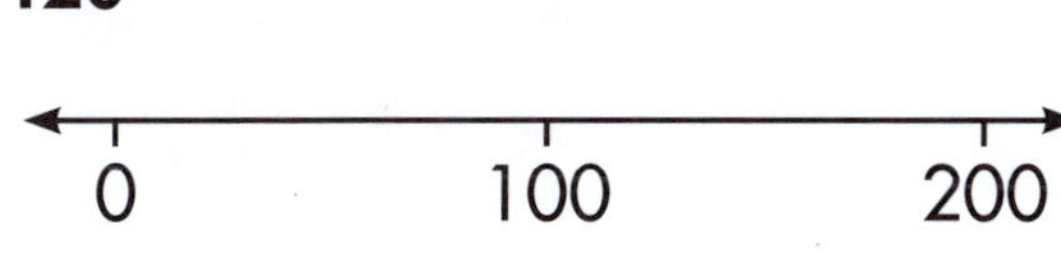

8 $\frac{1}{3}$

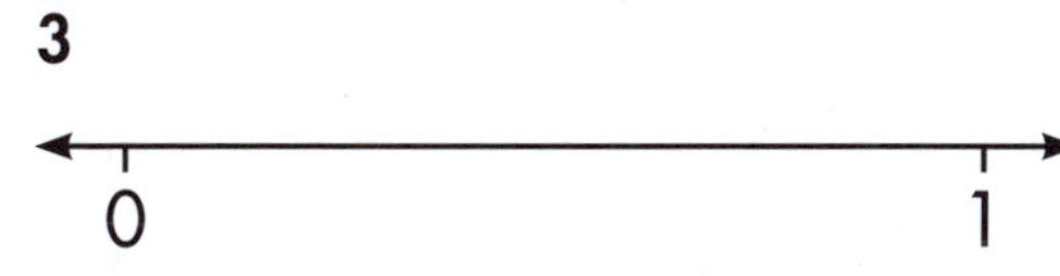

Problem solving

9 Sean wants to fill the jug to 2 L.
How much more juice does he need?

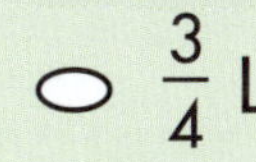 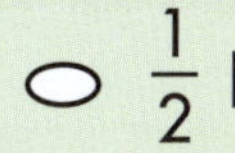

○ $\frac{3}{4}$ L ○ $\frac{1}{2}$ L ○ 1 L ○ $\frac{1}{3}$ L

BOB time!

ORDERING NUMBERS

Grouping can help you **order numbers** from smallest to largest.

53 47 41 57 48 50

Start with the highest place value (tens). Group numbers that have the same digit.

53 57 50 47 41 48

Use the digits in the next place value (ones) to order the numbers in each group from smallest to largest.

50 53 57 41 47 48

Put the groups in order.

41 47 48 50 53 57

Symbols help you compare numbers. They tell you whether a number is smaller, bigger or the same value as another number.

The < symbol means **less than**.

67 < 98 *67 is less than 98*

The > symbol means **greater than**.

56 > 31 *56 is greater than 31*

The = symbol means **is equal to** or **has the same value**.

87 = 87 *87 is equal to 87*

The pointy ends of the < and > symbols point to the smaller number!

Ordinal numbers tell you the order or position of numbers.

Here are some ordinal numbers: 1st, 2nd, 3rd, 22nd, 23rd, 24th.

The **third** star is green.

We practise

Order these numbers from largest to smallest: 165, 162, 261, 266, 163, 264.

261, 266, 264 165, 162, 163

266, 264, 261, 165, 163, 162

Write <, > or = in each box.

89 [>] 64 99 [<] 102 55 [=] 55

Draw a pattern using a circle as the 1st shape and 3rd shape, and a square as the 2nd shape and 4th shape.

Circle true or false.

1	58 > 35	True	False	2	670 = 670	True	False
3	7504 < 7409	True	False	4	137 > 173	True	False

Use the picture to answer the questions.

5 What position is the sleeping man in? ______

6 What position is the small child standing in? ______

7 What colour pants is the 7th person wearing? __________

8 If the lady reading the newspaper went home, what position would the small child be in then? ______

First look at the digits in the largest place value position.

Order the numbers from smallest to largest.

9 98, 100, 99, 101, 97 ____________________

10 906, 2005, 908, 2101, 2 ____________________

Order the numbers from largest to smallest.

11 401, 521, 411, 527, 418 ____________________

12 5745, 5645, 6645, 6745 ____________________

Problem solving

BOB time!

13 Six children had an ice cream eating race. Rank their times by writing their names in order from first place to sixth place.

Results: Jack = 102 sec, Neri = 133 sec, Otis = 120 sec, Jo = 112 sec, Maya = 98 sec, Zoe = 114 sec

1st	2nd	3rd	4th	5th	6th

FRACTIONS

Fractions are **parts of a whole.** Each fraction has a numerator and a denominator.

Numerator: The top number that tells you how many parts of the whole.

Denominator: The bottom number that tells you how many parts of the whole in total.

Some common fractions: $\frac{1}{2}, \frac{1}{3}, \frac{1}{4}, \frac{1}{5}, \frac{1}{6}, \frac{1}{10}$

This circle has been cut into 4 parts (denominator). 1 part (numerator) is coloured blue.
The fraction that is coloured blue is $\frac{1}{4}$.

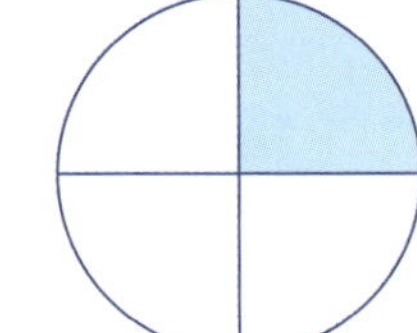

Fractions can describe groups of objects.

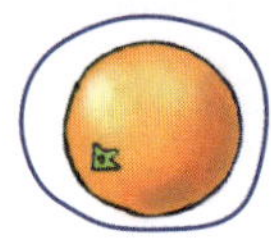  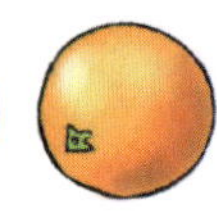 

1 of the 4 oranges is circled.
So $\frac{1}{4}$ of the group is circled.

When the **numerator** and the **denominator** are **the same**, the fraction equals **one whole**.

$\frac{5}{5} = 1$ $\frac{4}{4} = 1$

$\frac{2}{2} = 1$ $\frac{1}{1} = 1$

Mixed fractions are fractions that have both whole objects or numbers and parts of a whole (a fraction).

$1\frac{3}{4}$ 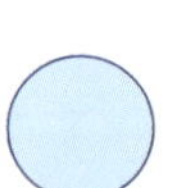 

We practise

Manue ate one piece of this chocolate bar.

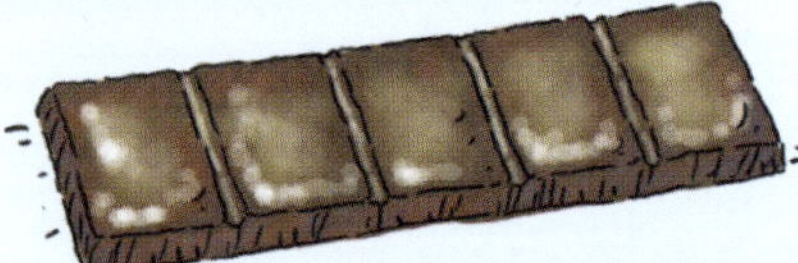

What fraction did she eat?

1 piece was eaten (numerator)
5 pieces in total (denominator)
Manue ate 1 out of the 5 pieces of the chocolate bar.
Manue ate $\frac{1}{5}$ of the chocolate bar.

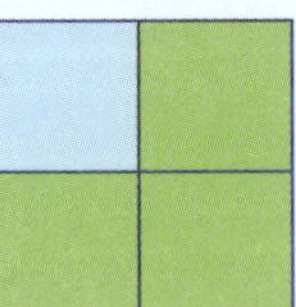

What fraction of the square is coloured blue? $\frac{1}{4}$

What fraction of the square is coloured green? $\frac{3}{4}$

What fraction of the group of pencils is circled?

3 out of the 4 pencils are circled, $\frac{3}{4}$.

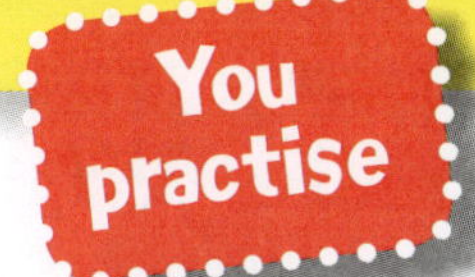

Write the fraction that is blue.

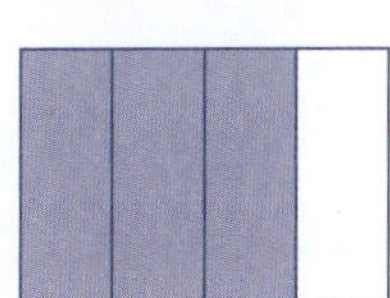
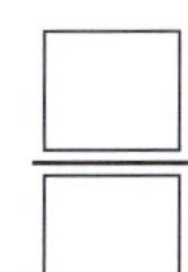
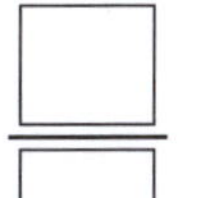
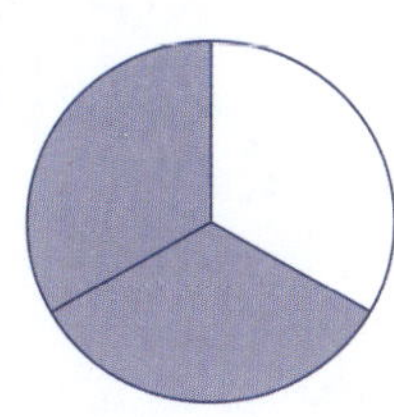

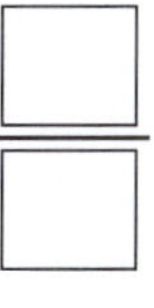

Colour the shapes to show these fractions.

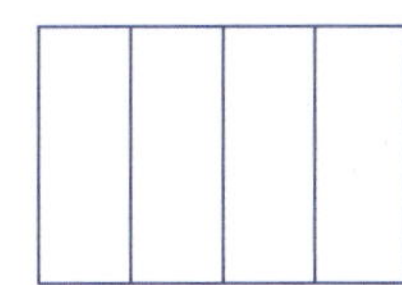
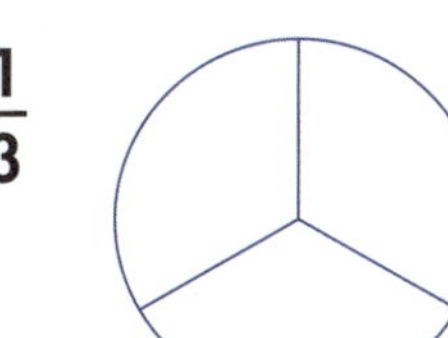

4 $\frac{1}{4}$ 5 $\frac{1}{3}$ 6 $\frac{1}{2}$

Write the fraction that is shown.

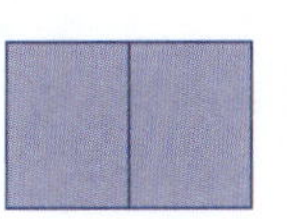
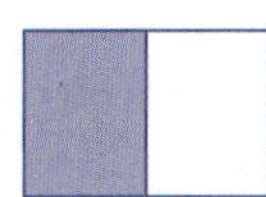
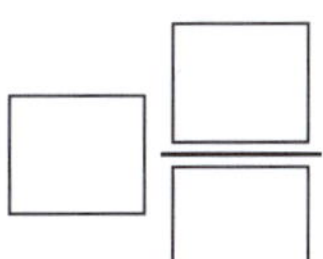
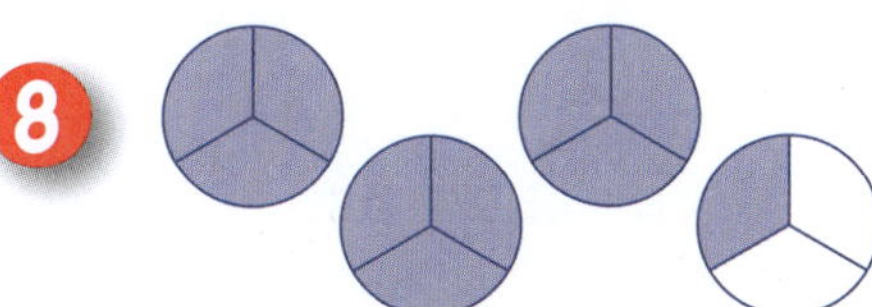
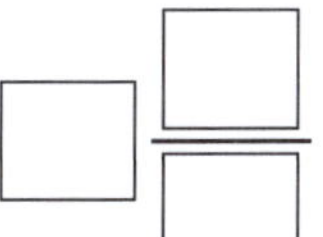

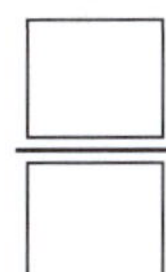

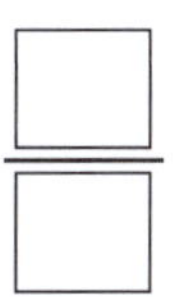

Circle part of the group to show these fractions.

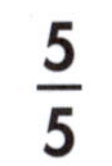

11 $\frac{1}{4}$ 12 $\frac{5}{5}$

13 $\frac{2}{6}$ 14 $\frac{3}{8}$

Problem solving

15 Abraham cut his birthday cake into 12 pieces. He and his three friends ate 2 pieces each. What fraction of the cake did they eat altogether?

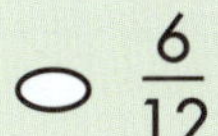
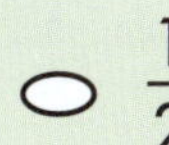

○ $\frac{6}{12}$ ○ $\frac{1}{2}$ ○ $\frac{8}{12}$ ○ $\frac{3}{12}$

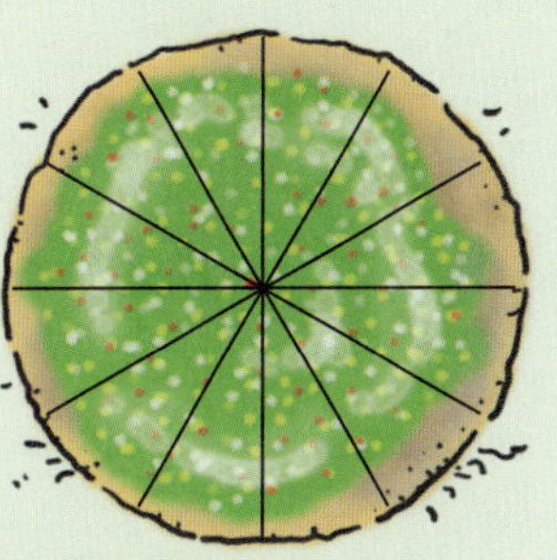

EQUIVALENT FRACTIONS

Equivalent fractions look different but have the **same value**.

To find an equivalent fraction, **multiply** the top number (**numerator**) and the bottom number (**denominator**) by the same number.

$$\frac{1}{2} = \frac{2}{4} = \frac{4}{8}$$

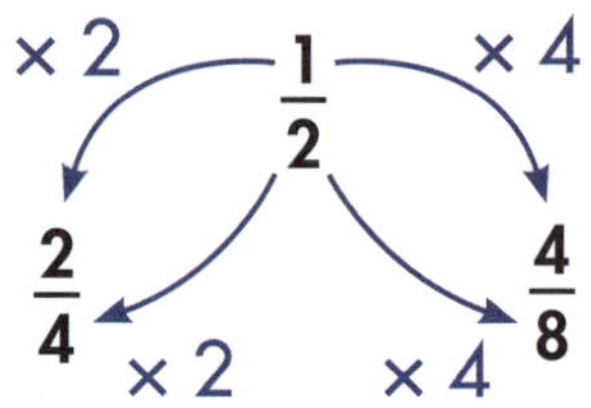

A **fraction wall** is a great way to look at equivalent fractions.

1

$\frac{1}{2}$	$\frac{1}{2}$

$\frac{1}{4}$	$\frac{1}{4}$	$\frac{1}{4}$	$\frac{1}{4}$

$\frac{1}{8}$	$\frac{1}{8}$	$\frac{1}{8}$	$\frac{1}{8}$	$\frac{1}{8}$	$\frac{1}{8}$	$\frac{1}{8}$	$\frac{1}{8}$

$\frac{1}{3}$	$\frac{1}{3}$	$\frac{1}{3}$

$\frac{1}{6}$	$\frac{1}{6}$	$\frac{1}{6}$	$\frac{1}{6}$	$\frac{1}{6}$	$\frac{1}{6}$

$\frac{1}{5}$	$\frac{1}{5}$	$\frac{1}{5}$	$\frac{1}{5}$	$\frac{1}{5}$

$\frac{1}{10}$	$\frac{1}{10}$	$\frac{1}{10}$	$\frac{1}{10}$	$\frac{1}{10}$	$\frac{1}{10}$	$\frac{1}{10}$	$\frac{1}{10}$	$\frac{1}{10}$	$\frac{1}{10}$

To **simplify** a fraction, divide the numerator and the denominator by the same number.

$$\frac{4}{8} = \frac{1}{2} \quad (\div 4)$$

$$\frac{3}{6} = \frac{1}{2} \quad (\div 3)$$

We practise

Complete the equivalent fractions. Use the fraction wall to help you.

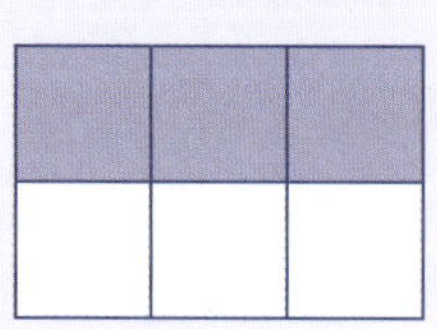

$\frac{1}{2} = \frac{3}{6}$ (× 3)

$\frac{1}{3} = \frac{2}{6}$ (× 2)

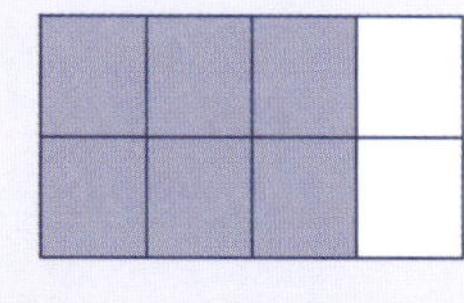

$\frac{3}{4} = \frac{6}{8}$ (× 2)

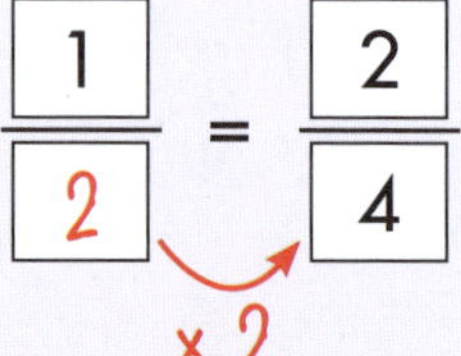

Write the equivalent fraction that matches the coloured part of each shape.

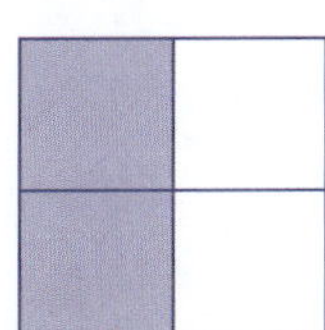

1. $\frac{1}{2} = \frac{\square}{4}$

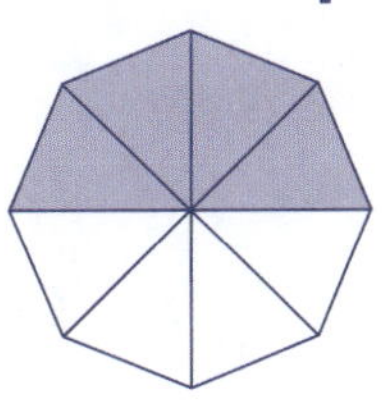

2. $\frac{1}{2} = \frac{\square}{8}$

Use the fraction wall to help you complete these equivalent fractions.

3. $\frac{1}{3} = \frac{\square}{6}$
4. $\frac{1}{4} = \frac{\square}{8}$
5. $\frac{1}{5} = \frac{\square}{10}$
6. $\frac{2}{5} = \frac{\square}{10}$
7. $\frac{3}{4} = \frac{\square}{8}$
8. $\frac{3}{3} = \frac{\square}{6}$

Draw a line to match each fraction to the picture that shows its equivalent fraction, then write the equivalent fraction.

9. $\frac{1}{3} = \frac{\square}{\square}$
10. $\frac{3}{6} = \frac{\square}{\square}$
11. $\frac{2}{3} = \frac{\square}{\square}$
12. $\frac{6}{8} = \frac{\square}{\square}$

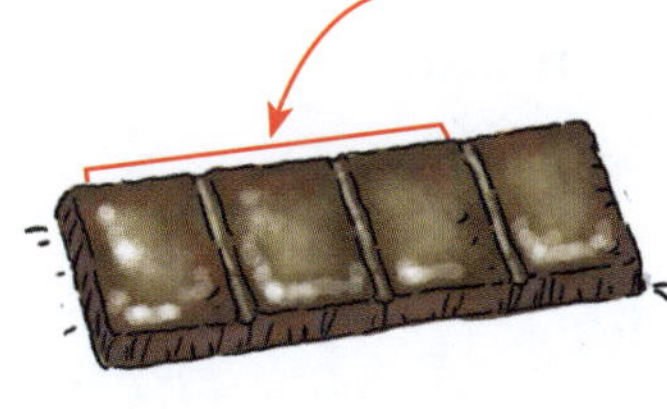
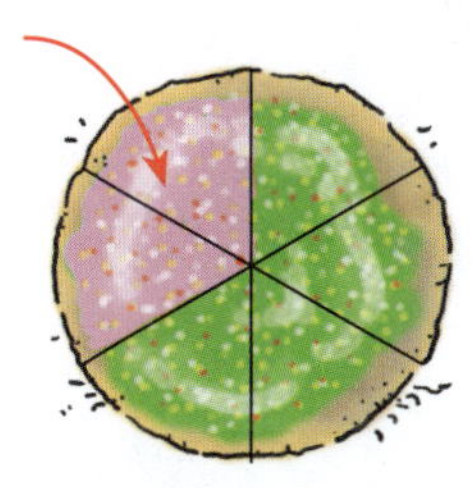

Problem solving

13. Lily cut her pizza into 12 pieces to share with her friends. She and her friends ate 9 pieces of it. What equivalent fraction did they eat?

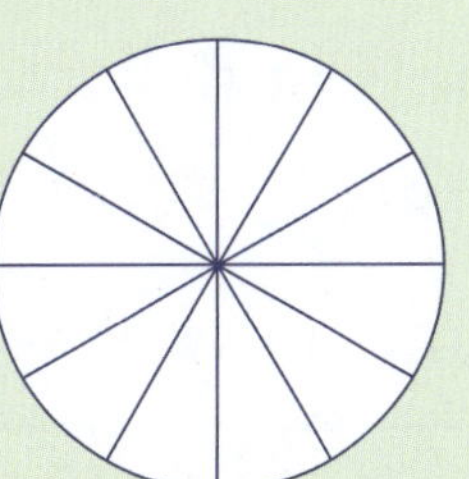

○ $\frac{3}{4}$ ○ $\frac{9}{9}$ ○ $\frac{3}{12}$ ○ $\frac{6}{9}$

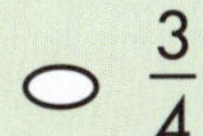

BOB time!

ADDING MONEY

Australian money is counted in dollars and cents. We use different coins and notes to represent different values.

5c, **10c**, **20c** and **50c** coins are silver coins. **$1** and **$2** coins are gold coins. Australian notes are made of plastic and come in **$5**, **$10**, **$20**, **$50** and **$100** values.

Use the right unit: $ or c, but not $ and c together!

Follow these steps to add the money.

1. **Group** the dollars together, then group the cents together.

2. **Order** the coins in each group from largest value to smallest value.

3. **Add** the dollars together, then add the cents together. **$2 + $1 = $3** **10c + 5c + 5c = 20c**

4. Add the dollars **total** to the cents total. The cents go after the decimal point, so $3 and 20c is $3.20. **$3 + 20c = $3.20**

Answer: $3.20

When you add money, you can divide by 100 to convert cents to dollars: 320c = $3.20

How much money does Rosie have?

= $1.00 + $1.00 + 50c + 20c + 20c + 5c
= $2.00 + 95c
= $2.95
Rosie has $2.95.

We practise

Write these amounts in dollars.

120c = $1.20   80c = $0.80

Write these amounts in cents.

$0.50 = 50c $2.00 = 200c

Total each child's money to find out who saved the most.

1 Toby

Total:

2 Giselle

Total:

3 Allie

Total:

4 Pavan

Total:

5 Who saved the most money? ______________

Draw each amount using the fewest number of coins.

6 \$2.50

7 \$1.85

8 \$4.15

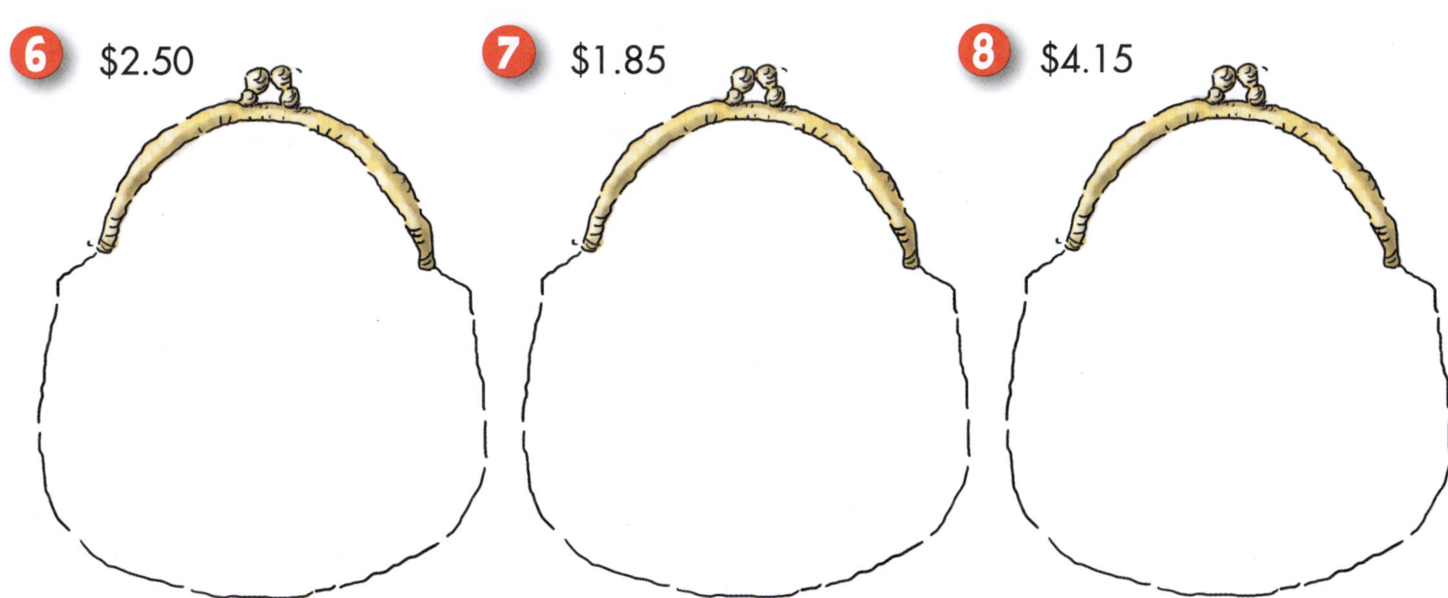

Problem solving

9 Clay is going to the carnival.
How much money has he got?

- ⬭ \$3.50
- ⬭ \$3.45
- ⬭ \$2.50
- ⬭ \$3.55

BOB time!

MONEY – CHANGE

You get **change** when you pay more money than you need to when you buy something.

Jack uses a **$5 note** to buy some juice that **costs $1.70**.
You can use a **number line** to find out how much change Jack will get.

Start with the cost of the juice.

Count up in cents to the next dollar.

Count up in dollars to the amount paid.

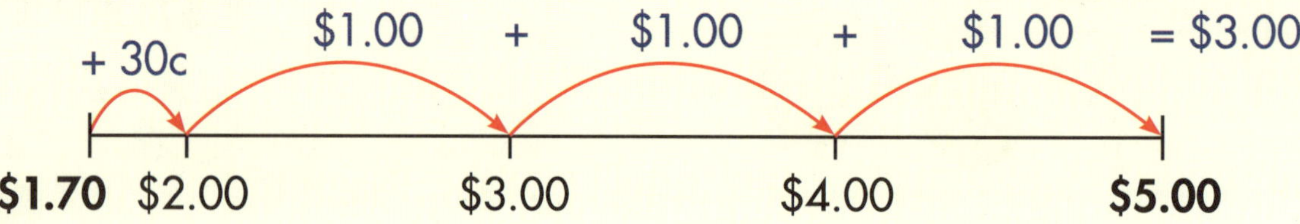

Add the cents to the dollars: **30c + $3.00 = $3.30**

Answer: Jack's change is $3.30.

Use the units $ or c in your answer.

First count up in cents to the next dollar, then count up in dollars!

Mick uses a $5 note to pay for a sandwich that costs $2.30. How much change will he get?

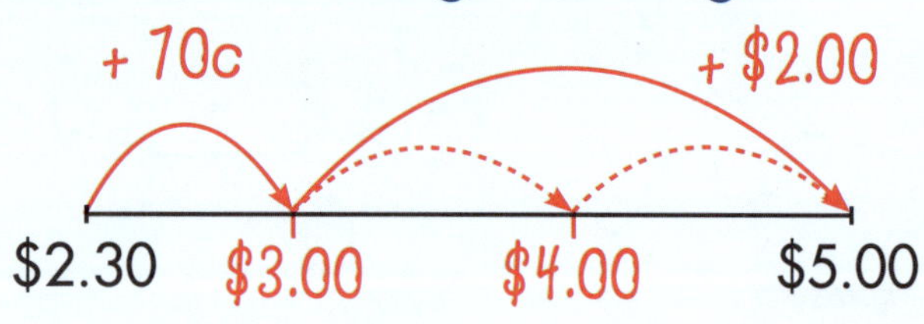

$5.00 - $2.30
= 70c + $2.00
= $2.70
Mick will get $2.70 change.

We practise

Sara uses a $10 note to buy a frisbee that costs $6.90. How much change will she get?

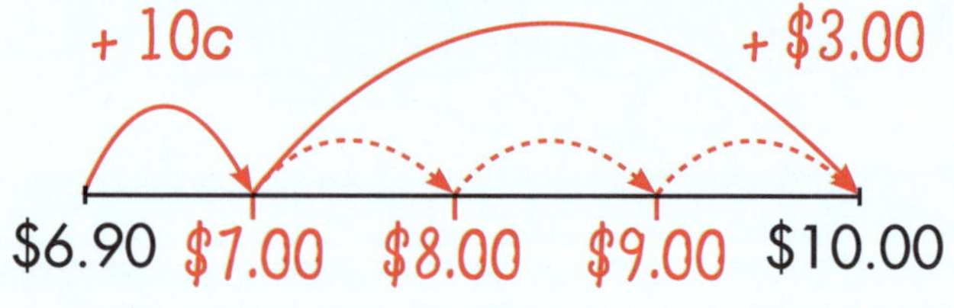

$10.00 - $6.90
= 10c + $3.00
= $3.10
Sara will get $3.10 change.

You practise

How much change do you get?
Use the number lines to work it out.

1. A book costs $3.15 and you pay $5.

85c

$3.15 $4.00

Change: $

2. A necklace costs $2.75 and you pay $5.

Change: $

3. A toy car costs $5.45 and you pay $10.

Change: $

4. A hat costs $8.75 and you pay $10.

Change: $

See if you can work these out in your head, following the same steps.

5. A hot chocolate costs $3.60 and you pay $5.00. Change: $______
6. An ice cream costs $2.25 and you pay $5.00. Change: $______
7. A bus ticket costs $6.45 and you pay $10.00. Change: $______
8. A school hat costs $8.15 and you pay $10.00. Change: $______

Problem solving

9. One lollipop costs 50c.
Kira buys 3 lollipops and pays with a $5.00 note.
How much change does she get?

Change: $______

BOB time!

LENGTH, MASS and CAPACITY

MEASUREMENT & GEOMETRY

You can measure the length, mass and capacity of any object.

When you measure:

- line up your object with the zero on the measuring device.
- check the **intervals** of the measuring tool
- don't forget the **units**: **cm**, **m**, **mL**, **L**, **g** or **kg**.

Conversion means changing units from **bigger to smaller** or **smaller to bigger**.

Common conversions

Length:
1 km = 1000 m
1 m = 100 cm
1 cm = 10 mm

Mass:
1 kg = 1000 g

Capacity:
1 L = 1000 mL

To convert cm ↔ m: divide or multiply by 100.

To convert g ↔ kg, mL ↔ L and m ↔ km: divide or multiply by 1000.

The **length** of an object is **how long** it is.

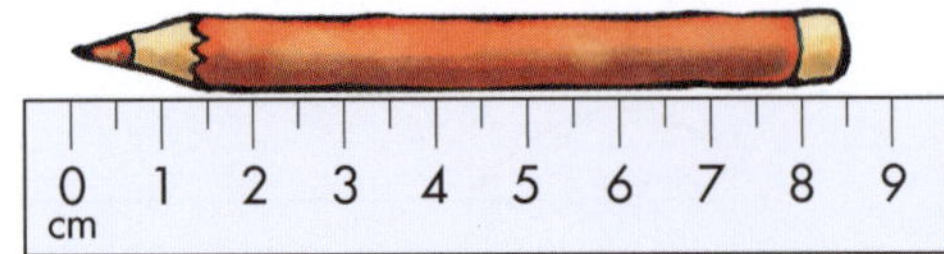

This pencil is 8.5 cm in length.

The **mass** of an object is **how heavy** it is.

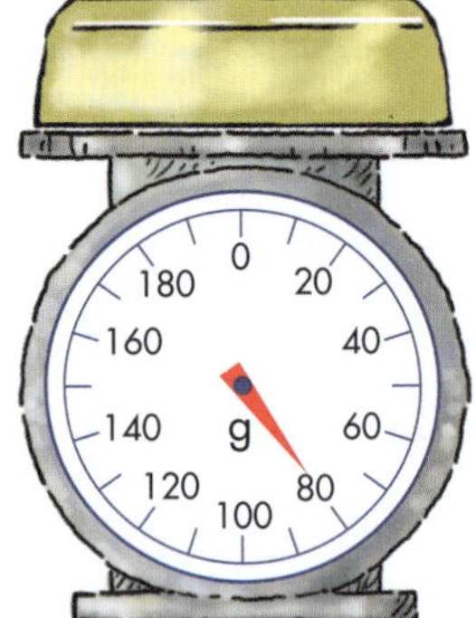

This gold weighs 80 g.

The **capacity** of an object is **how much** liquid it holds.

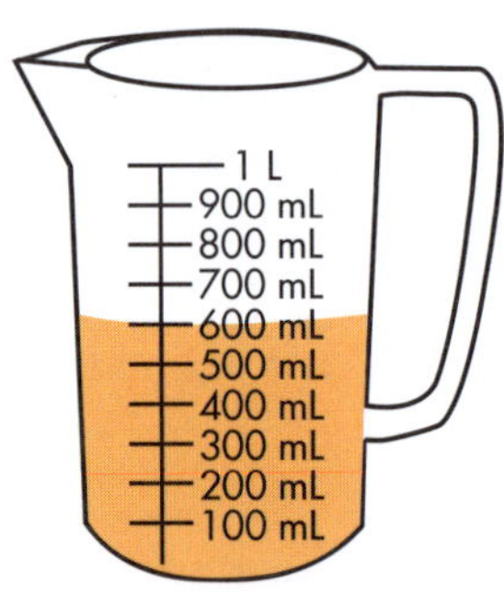

This jug can hold 1 L. It is holding 600 mL of juice.

Convert 2500 metres to kilometres.

Split the number up.

2500 m = 2000 m + 500 m

Use your conversion knowledge.

2000 m = 2 km

Answer: 2500 = 2 km and 500 m
= 2.5 km

We practise

What is the weight of the clock?

The clock weighs 80 g.

Convert 5250 millilitres to litres.

5250 mL = 5000 mL + 250 mL
(5000 mL = 5 L) (250 mL = 0.25 L)
5250 mL = 5 L and 0.25 mL = 5.25 L

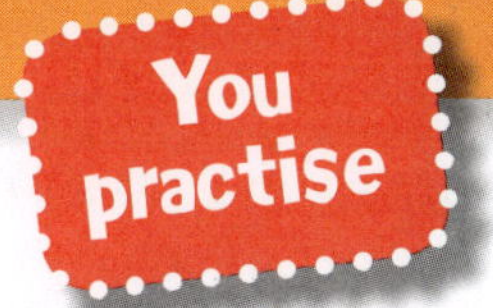

Measure these objects.

3

0 1 2 3 4 5 6 7 8 9 10 11 12 13 14 15 cm

__________ __________ __________

Divide by 100 to convert these centimetre measurements to metres. For example, 375 cm = 3.75 m.

4 180 cm = ________ m

5 459 cm = ________ m

6 5682 cm = ________ m

Convert these measurements. Be careful with the units – check the unit conversion facts!

7 5690 g = ________ kg

8 4.2 L = ________ mL

9 2.93 km = ________ m

10 252 mm = ________ cm

11 9266 m = ________ km

12 5.71 kg = ________ g

Problem solving

13 How long is this pencil case?

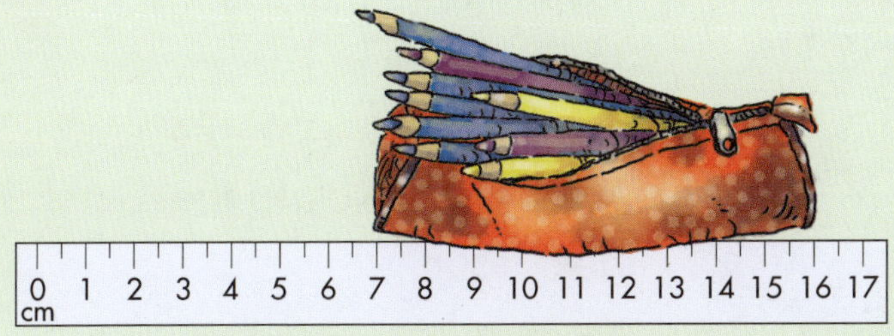

- ○ 10 cm
- ○ 7 cm
- ○ 16 cm
- ○ 9 cm

How much ice cream is in the container?

- ○ 1.2 L
- ○ 12.0 L
- ○ 120 L
- ○ 0.12 L

BOB time!

TIME

An **analogue clock** has two hands.

The **long hand** is the minute hand and tells you the number of **minutes**.

The **short hand** is the hour hand and tells you the number of **hours**.

Time facts!

60 minutes = 1 hour
24 hours = 1 day
12 midnight to 11.59 am = am
12 noon to 11.59 pm = pm

Find the time past the hour.

Count in 5s then 1s from the 0 minute to the long hand.

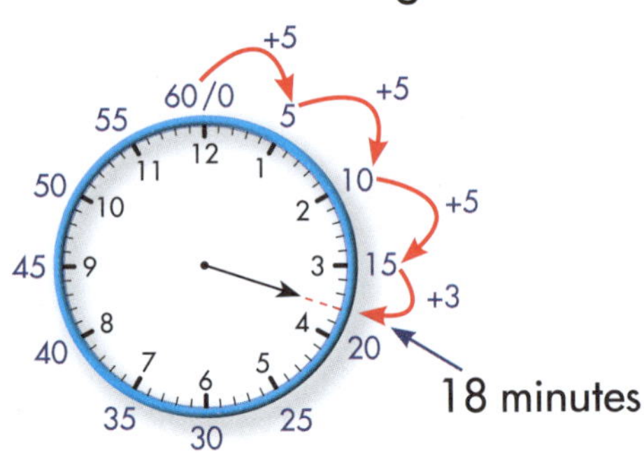

Find the number the short hand has passed.

It is 18 minutes past 2.

Find the time to the hour.

When the long hand is past the 6, work backwards from the o'clock.

It is 12 minutes to 7.

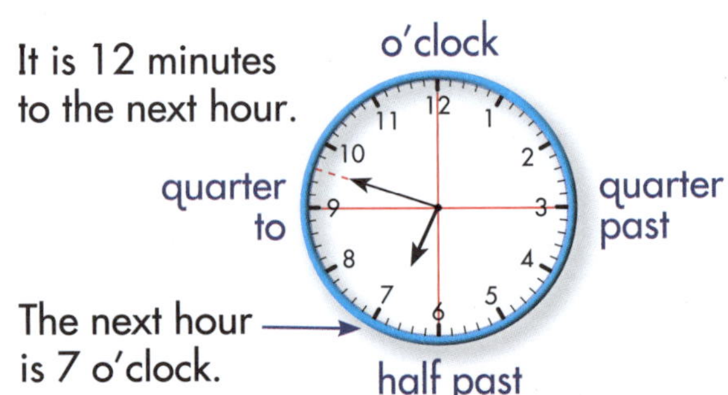

On a **digital clock**, the left side shows the hour.

The right side always shows the minutes **past the hour**.

18 minutes past 2: 2:18

12 minutes to 7: 6:48

We practise

Write the 'to the hour' time and show it on the digital clock.

+ 3
+ 5
+ 5
+ 5
+ 5

12:37

Count in 1s then 5s to the o'clock:

3 + 5 + 5 + 5 + 5 = 23

It is 23 minutes to the next hour.

The hour hand is between 12 and 1.

The time is 23 minutes to 1.

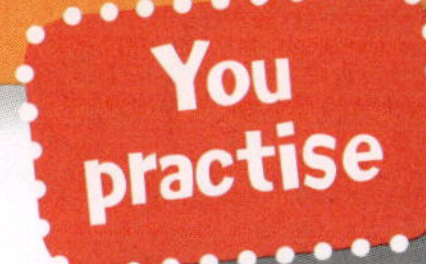

Write the 'past the hour' time and show it on the digital clock.

2

3

Write the 'to the hour' time and and show it on the digital clock.

4

5

6

Show the time on the clock face and the digital clock.

7 Quarter to 8

8 Half past 11

9 Quarter past 4

Remember to make the **hour hand** shorter than the **minute hand**!

Problem solving

10 The clock shows the starting time of the concert. What time is it?

- 8:40
- 8:36
- 36:8
- 7:36

BOB time!

CALENDARS and TIMETABLES

A **calendar** tells you what day and month it is.

MARCH						
Sun	Mon	Tues	Wed	Thur	Fri	Sat
						1
2	3	4	5	6	7	8
9	10	11	12	13	14	15
16	17	18	19	20	21	22
23	24	25	26	27	28	29
30	31					

Sunday is the start of the week.

This is 1 week.

This month has 5 Mondays!

The **month** is March, the **day of the week** is Friday and the **date** is the 21st.

The first day of this month is a Saturday.

The last day of this month is a Monday.

A **timetable** tells you when something starts, finishes, arrives or departs.

Here is the **title**.

Athletics carnival			
Event	Yr 1	Yr 2	Yr 3
Sprint	9:05	9:10	9:15
Long jump	10:05	10:10	10:15
High jump	11:05	11:10	11:15
Sack race	12:05	12:10	12:15

Events **start** at these times.

Use the calendar to answer the questions.

SEPTEMBER						
S	M	T	W	T	F	S
			1	2	3	4
5	6	7	8	9	10	11
12	13	14	15	16	17	18
19	20	21	22	23	24	25
26	27	28	29	30		

What day is the 22nd?

Wednesday

How many Saturdays are there? 4

Use the timetable to answer the questions.

Movies		
Movie	Start	Finish
Star Wars	11:00	12:30
Spy Kids	11:30	1:00
Pony Club	2:00	4:00

How long is the movie Pony Club?

2 hours

Which movie starts at 11:00?

Star Wars

We practise

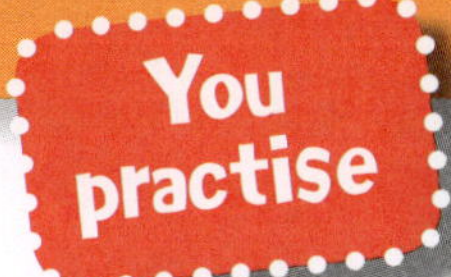

Use the calendar to answer these questions.

MAY						
Sun	Mon	Tues	Wed	Thur	Fri	Sat
	1	2	3	4	5	6 soccer
7	8	9 Dad's b-day	10	11	12	13
14	15	16	17	18	19	20
21	22 ballet	23	24	25	26	27
28	29	30	31			

1. What is the date of the third Wednesday of the month?

   ____

2. How many Fridays are there in this month?

   ____

3. What date is Dad's birthday?

   ____

4. What day of the week is ballet?

   ____

5. What day is the first day of the **next** month? ____________________

Use the timetable to answer these questions.

Flights from Brisbane Airport		
Destination	Departs	Arrives
Sydney	9:00 am	10:35 am
Hobart	6:00 am	11:30 am
Cairns	7:00 am	9:30 am
Melbourne	8:00 am	10:00 am
Canberra	9:00 am	10:00 am

6. How long is the flight from Brisbane to Cairns? ____ h _____ min
7. The Melbourne flight is delayed by 1 hour. When does it depart? ________
8. Cara is 2 hours early for the flight to Hobart. What time did she arrive at the airport? ________
9. Lee is flying to Sydney and Mia is flying to Canberra. Who will arrive first? ______

Problem solving

10. Tim catches the bus to school every morning. It takes him 10 minutes to walk to the bus stop. What time does he need to leave home to get to school before 9 am?

    ____

School Bus timetable	
Departs	Arrives
8:35 am	8:50 am
8:50 am	9:05 am

BOB time!

COORDINATES

Coordinates are a method of pinpointing an exact position on a grid.

They use the **horizontal line** and **vertical line** and their corresponding numbers or letters to guide you to the right position.

- **Reading coordinates** — read the horizontal line first, then the vertical line.
- **Writing coordinates** — write the horizontal letter first, then the vertical number.
- **Marking coordinates** — put your finger on the points at each line or space, then bring them together until they meet.

First go across, then go up – like a plane!

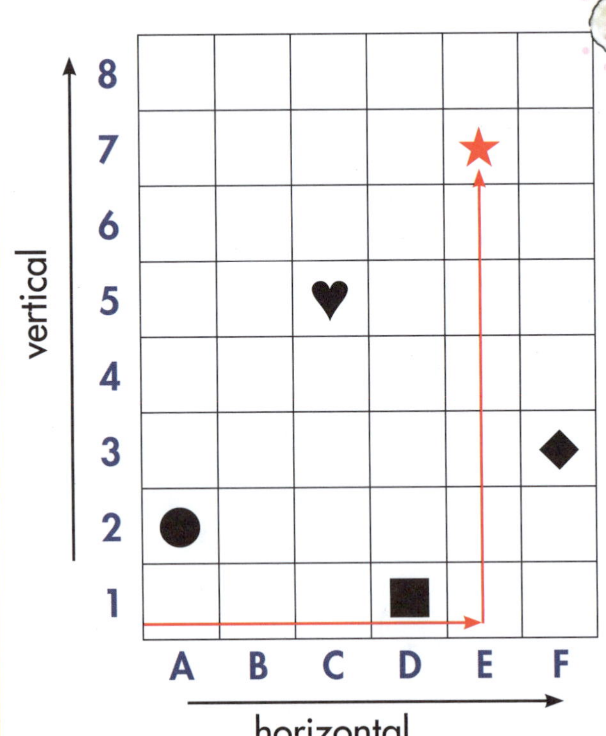

What are the coordinates for the star?

Go along the **horizontal line** to see how far **across** it is.

horizontal = E

Go up the **vertical line** to see how far **up** it is.

vertical = 7

Answer: E7

What are the coordinates for the pirate's gold?

horizontal line = F

vertical line = 1

Answer: F1

We practise

**Here is a plan of 3B's classroom.
Write the coordinates for these objects.**

1. Teacher's desk: __ __
2. Computer: __ __
3. Green table: __ __
4. Library corner: __ __
5. Rug: __ __ and __ __
6. Whiteboard: __ __ and __ __
7. Red table: __ __
8. Art area: __ __ and __ __

	A	B	C	D	E	F
6	whiteboard					
5			rug			
4						
3						
2						
1						

Find the coordinates on the grid and write the corresponding letters to spell out two words.

9.

B5	C1	F6	E2

G8	C7	A2	D4

	A	B	C	D	E	F	G
8		Z					W
7	S		O		Q		
6				C		O	
5		G					F
4	N			K		L	
3			B				
2	R				D		
1			O				M

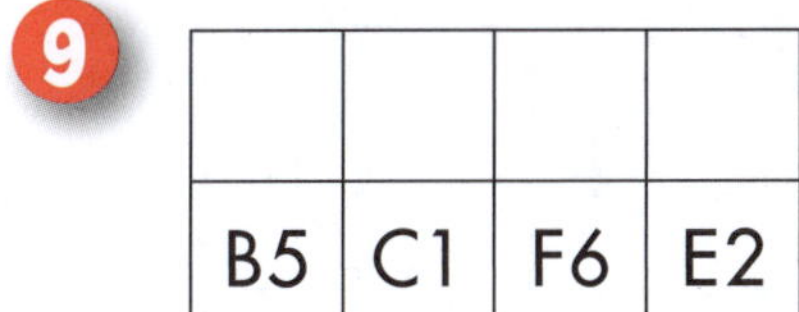

Problem solving

10. Look at 3B's classroom plan at the top of this page.
If the teacher's desk is moved 3 squares to the left, what are its new coordinates?

○ F4 ○ F1 ○ C4 ○ 4C

POSITION

You can find the **position** of an object or give a **direction** by using compass points (North, South, East and West), by turning set angles **clockwise** or **anticlockwise**, or by using words such as left or right.

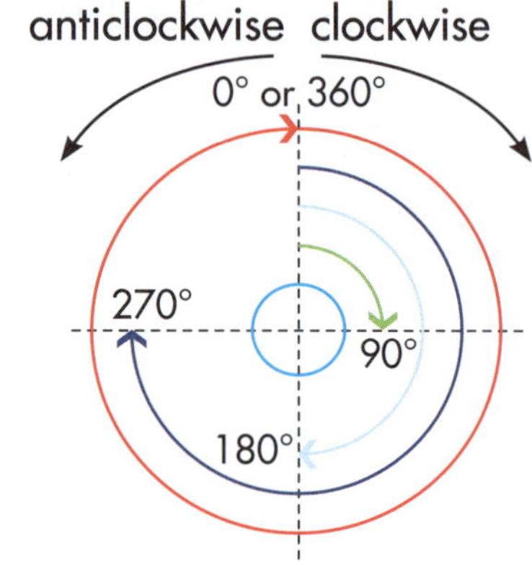

90° = *quarter turn*
180° = *half turn*
270° = *three-quarter turn*
360° = *full turn*

An **intersection** is where two roads or paths meet or cross.

Give directions from the green dot to the red dot.

1. From the green dot, head **North** following Baker Street until you reach the **intersection** with Gattney Street.
2. **Turn 90° anticlockwise** and go **straight** along Gattney Street.
3. **Follow** Gattney Street until the Campbell Street **intersection**.
4. **Turn 90°** to the **North** on to Campbell Street.
5. **Stop** at the Campbell Street and Walker Street **intersection**.
6. Go **East** along Walker Street until you reach the South Gate of Centenary Park.
7. Go **North** through Centenary Park until you reach the red dot.

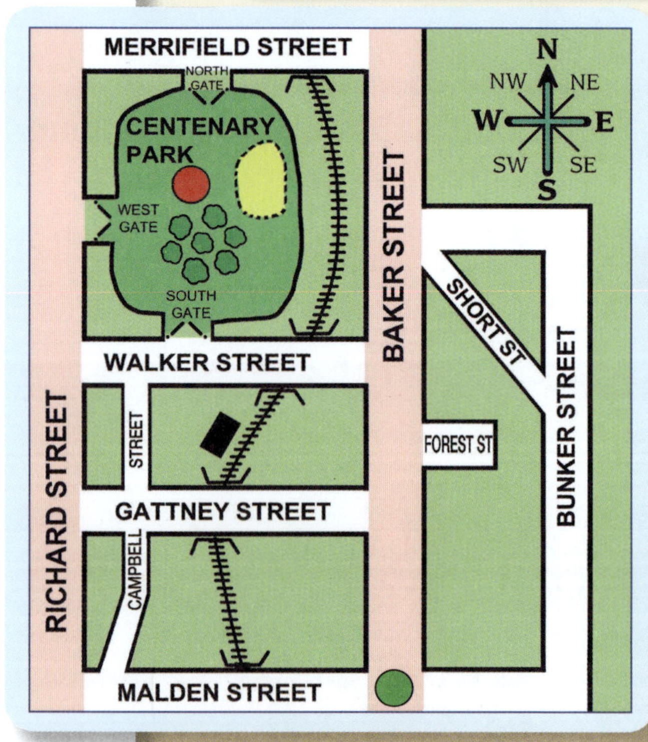

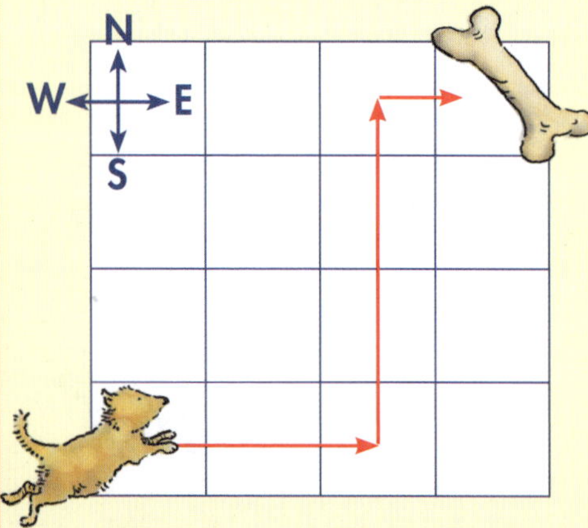

Write directions to help the dog find the bone.

1. Go East two squares.
2. Turn 90° anticlockwise to the North.
3. Go straight ahead three squares.
4. Turn to the East and go forward until you find the bone.

We practise

Use the map to answer these position questions.

1. What is North of the eating area?

   ____

2. When you travel West from the cricket pitch, what building do you get to?

   ____

3. What building is just South of the Prep playground?

   ____

Prep playground		N W E S	Tennis courts
Prep classroom	Pool		
Year 3 classroom			Cricket pitch
Year 2 classroom		Oval	
Hall	Eating area		

Where do you arrive when you follow these instructions?

4. Start at the Year 2 classroom. Go North. Turn right at the Year 3 classroom and go forward until you reach the cricket pitch. Make a quarter turn anticlockwise and move forward two squares.

   Arrive at: ______________________

5. Start at the tennis courts and go West three squares. Turn 270° clockwise and go straight ahead until you reach the hall. Make a quarter turn anticlockwise and go ahead one square.

   Arrive at: ______________________

6. Start at the eating area and go East two squares. Turn 90° anticlockwise and go straight ahead two squares.

   Arrive at: ______________________

Problem solving

7. Look at the map above. Jack wants to walk from the pool to the hall. What directions would you give him?

- ○ Go South three squares. Turn 90° clockwise and go straight ahead.
- ○ Make a half turn clockwise. Head South two squares, then turn right.
- ○ Go North three squares. Turn left and move forward two squares.
- ○ Make a three-quarter turn anticlockwise. Turn right, then head South.

SYMMETRY

An object, shape or picture has a line of symmetry when each side matches exactly when it is folded along a line. The fold line is the line of symmetry.

This type of symmetry is also known as **reflective symmetry**. If a mirror can be placed on a shape and shows an exact reflection of the other half of the shape, it has symmetry. The **mirror line** is the line of symmetry.

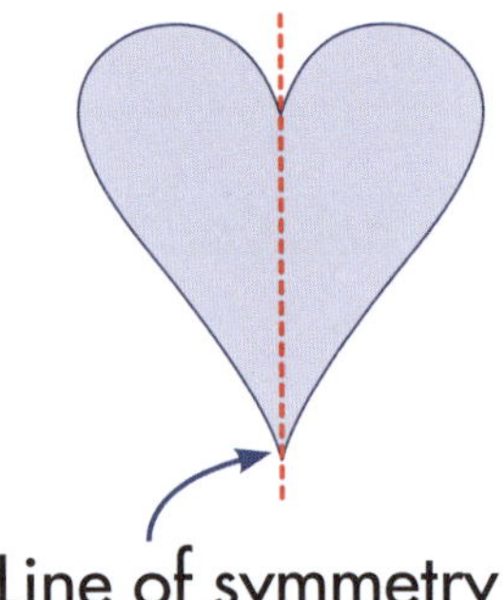

Line of symmetry or mirror line

To find out if a shape has a line of symmetry, fold the shape in half and see if it matches exactly.

This shape has one line of symmetry.

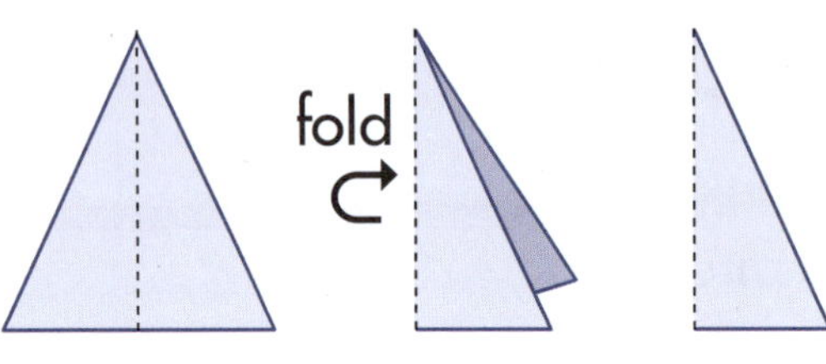

This shape does not have a line of symmetry.

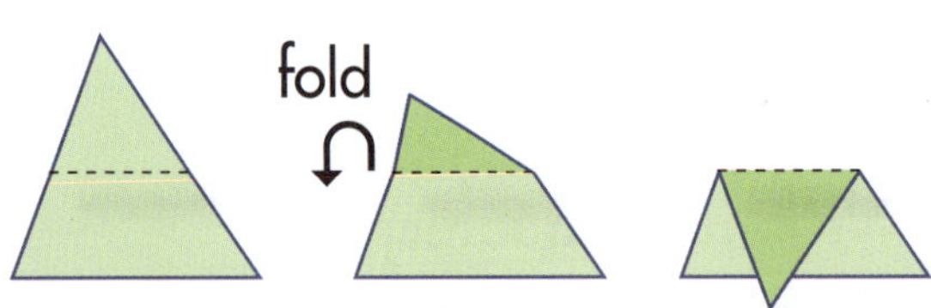

Some shapes have more than one line of symmetry.

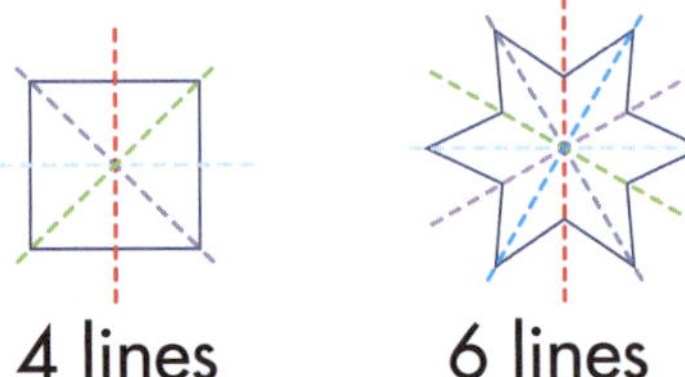

4 lines 6 lines

Some shapes have no lines of symmetry.

Transformation means to change a shape's position without changing the shape itself. Flip, slide and turn are types of transformations.

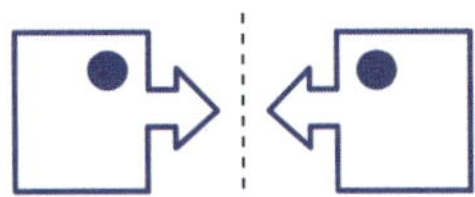

Flip: to turn over across a straight line

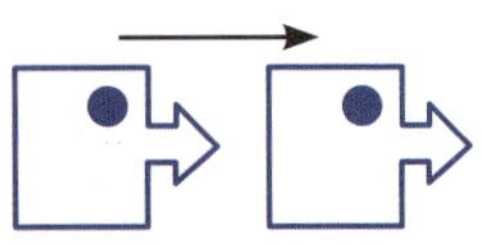

Slide: to move any direction without lifting

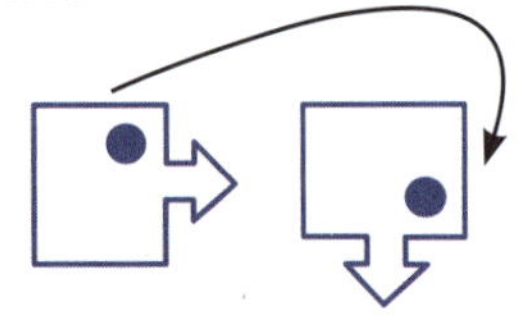

Turn: to turn or rotate

How many lines of symmetry does each shape have?

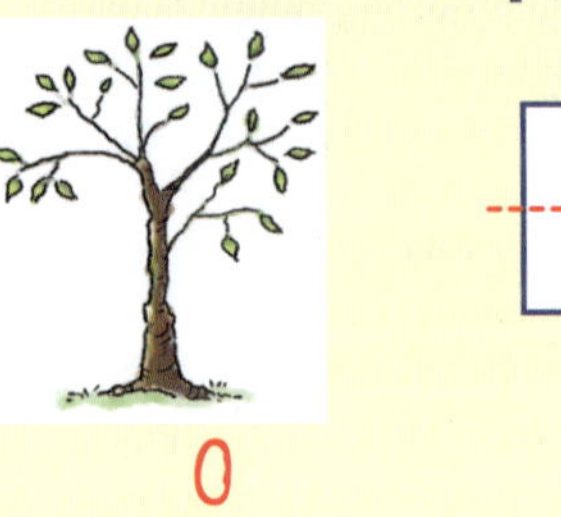

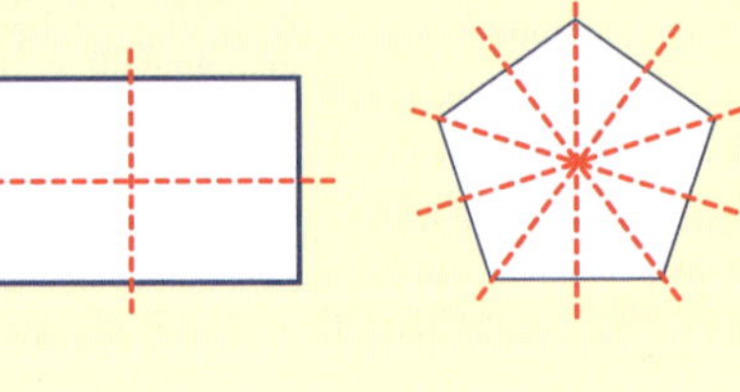

0 2 5

Flip this shape vertically.

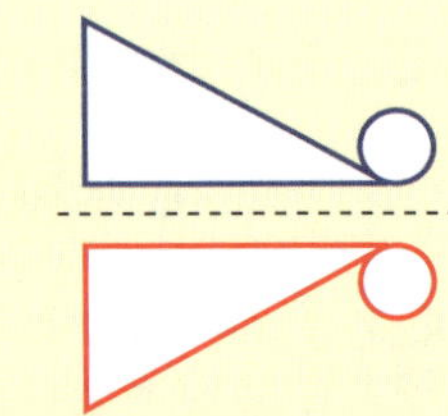

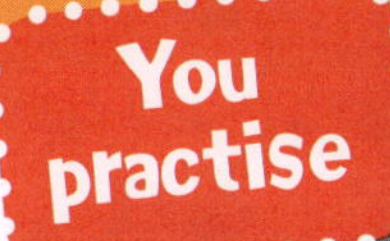

Join the lines of symmetry to their correct shapes.

1 0 lines of symmetry

2 1 line of symmetry

3 2 lines of symmetry

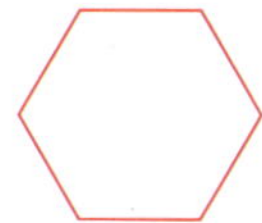     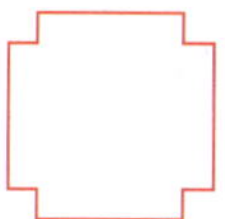

4 3 lines of symmetry

5 4 lines of symmetry

6 6 lines of symmetry

Follow the instructions and draw the shapes in their new positions.

7 Slide

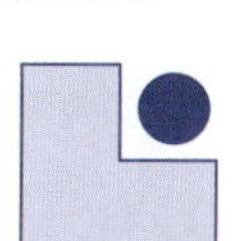

8 Flip horizontally

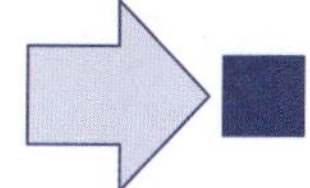

9 Three-quarter turn clockwise

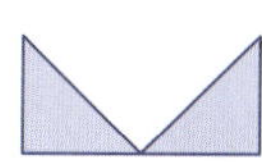

Draw the reflection to make each shape symmetrical.

10 

11 

12 

How many sides and lines of symmetry do the shapes have? What is the pattern?

13 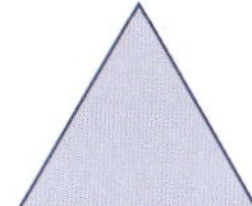
Sides: ____
Lines of symmetry: ____

14 
Sides: ____
Lines of symmetry: ____

15 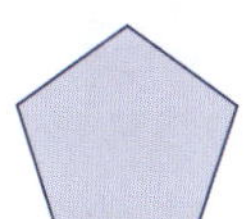
Sides: ____
Lines of symmetry: ____

16 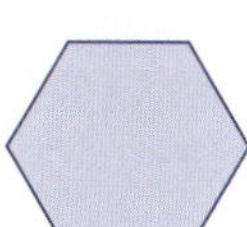
Sides: ____
Lines of symmetry: ____

17 Pattern: ______________________________

Problem solving

18 Circle the numerals that have at least one line of symmetry.

0 1 2 3 4 5 6 7 8 9

BOB time!

2D SHAPES

Two-dimensional shapes are flat or plane shapes with **sides** that join to make a closed shape. Most 2D shapes are **polygons**.
A polygon is any 2D shape that has three or more straight sides. Polygons can be further grouped into the following categories:

Regular polygons have sides of equal lengths.

Equilateral triangle
3 sides

Square
4 sides

Pentagon
5 sides

Hexagon
6 sides

Heptagon
7 sides

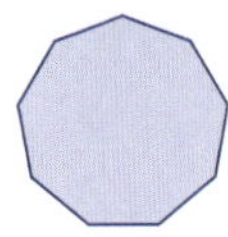
Octagon
8 sides

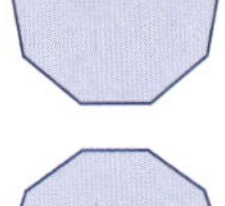
Nonagon
9 sides

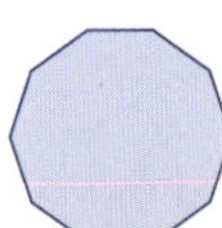
Decagon
10 sides

Irregular polygons have sides of different lengths.

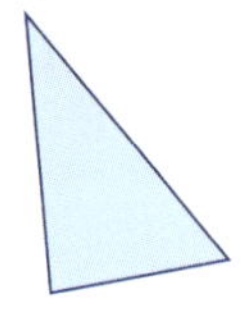
Scalene triangle
3 sides
all different lengths

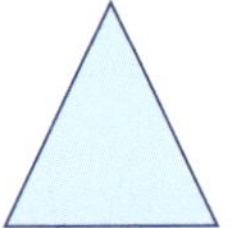
Isosceles triangle
3 sides
2 sides the same length

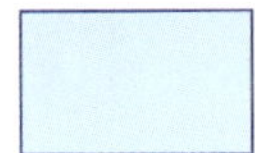
Rectangle
4 sides

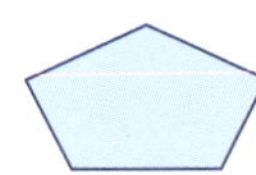
Irregular pentagon
5 sides

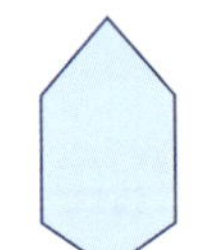
Irregular hexagon
6 sides

Non-polygons have sides that are curved, not straight.

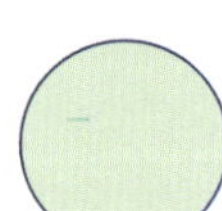
Circle
1 side

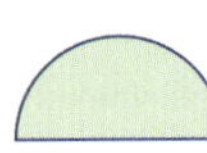
Semi-circle
2 sides

To check if a shape is a regular polygon, see if the sides are equal in length.

An irregular pentagon has 5 sides of different lengths.

We practise

Name the regular polygon that matches the number of sides.

7 sides: heptagon
10 sides: decagon
6 sides: hexagon
5 sides: pentagon
8 sides: octagon
9 sides: nonagon

Circle the irregular pentagons.

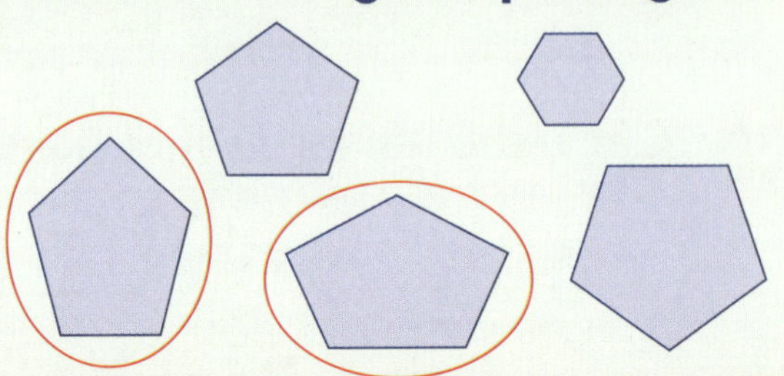

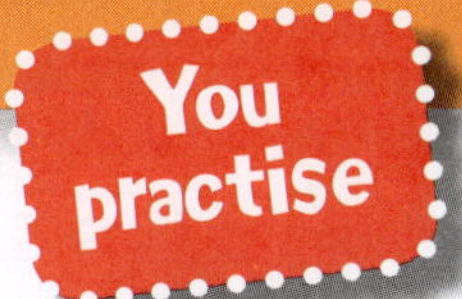

Name these regular polygons.

1  ______________________

2  ______________________

3 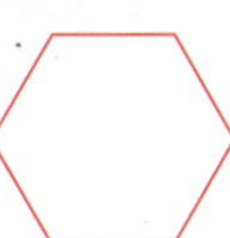 ______________________

Name these irregular polygons.

4 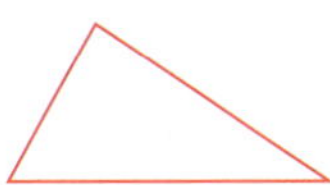 ______________________

5  ______________________

6 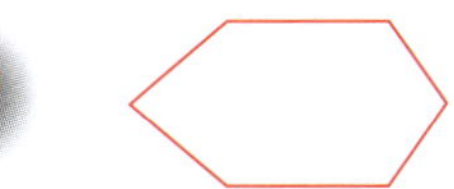 ______________________

Circle the matching shape.

7 heptagon

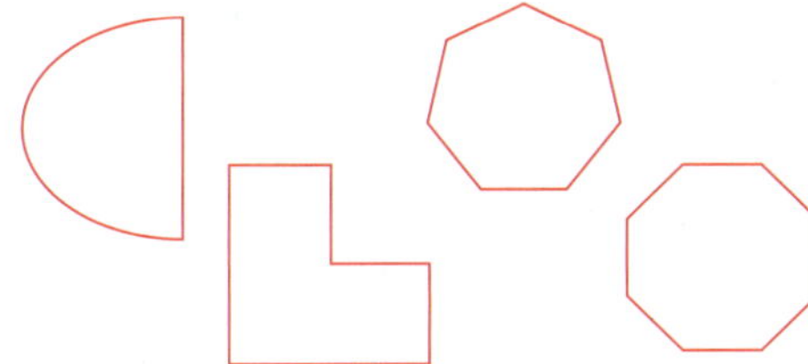

8 non-polygon

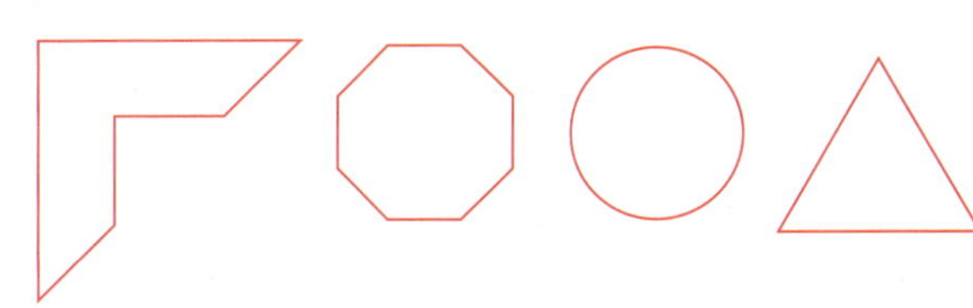

Write the number of sides and draw the 2D shape.

9 octagon
_____ sides

10 isosceles triangle
_____ sides

11 semi-circle
_____ sides

Problem solving

12 How many triangles are there in this picture?

_____ triangles

3D OBJECTS

Three-dimensional objects are solid shapes with height, width and depth.

3D objects have:

- **faces** (flat surfaces)
- **edges** (where two faces meet)
- **vertices** (points where edges meet).

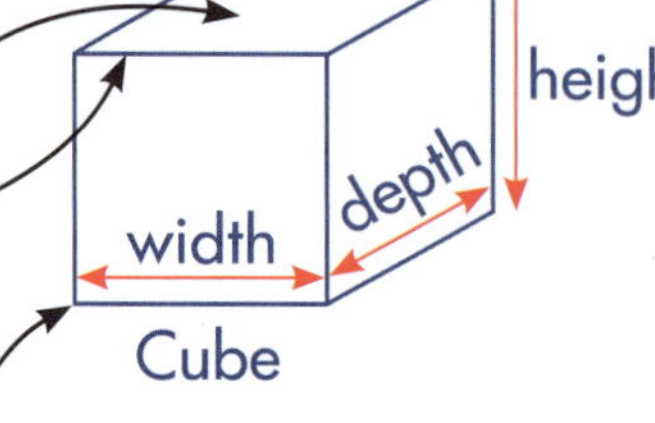

A curved surface counts as one face.

Sphere

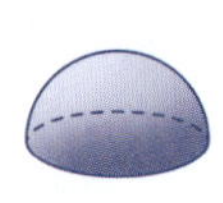
Hemisphere

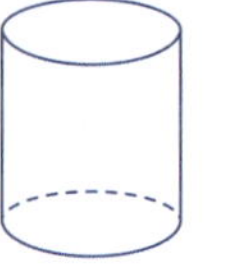
Cylinder

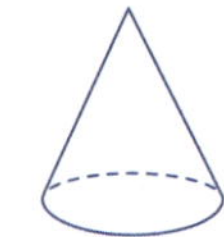
Cone

A sphere does not have edges or vertices.

The names of **prisms** come from the shape of the two identical faces at each end. The other faces are always **rectangles**.

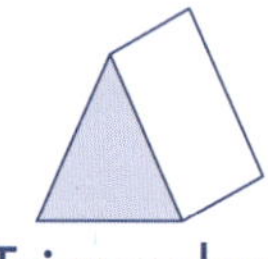
Triangular prism

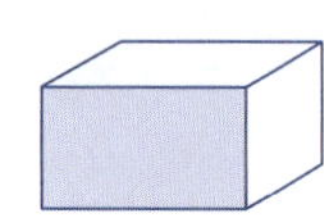
Rectangular prism

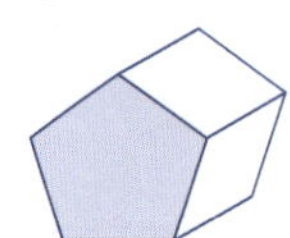
Pentagonal prism

The names of **pyramids** come from the shape of the base. The other faces that meet at a point (vertex) are always **triangles**.

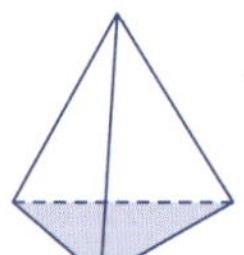
Triangular pyramid

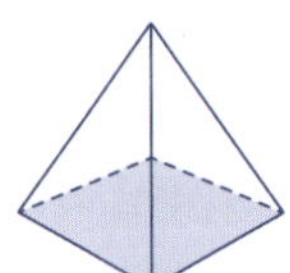
Square-based pyramid

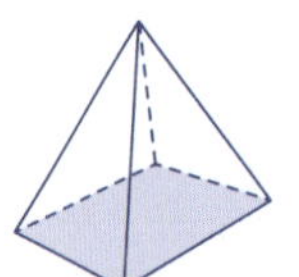
Rectangular pyramid

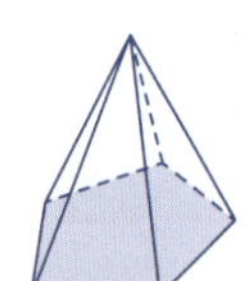
Pentagonal pyramid

A net is a pattern you can fold to make a 3D object.

Some 3D objects have only one net. Others have many nets.

Nets of a cube

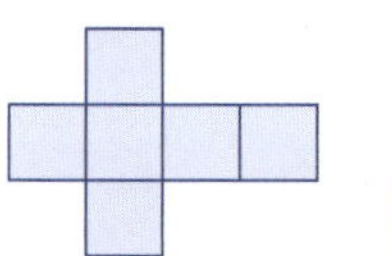

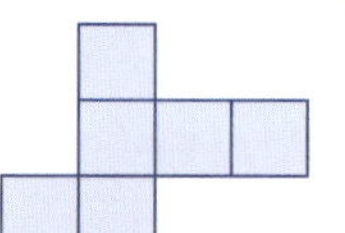

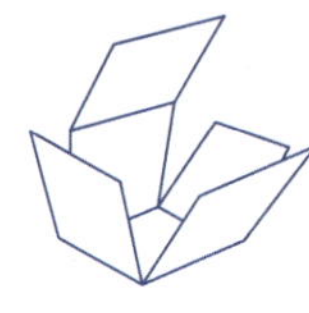

When a 3D object is cut through the middle, the 2D shape you see is called the cross-section.

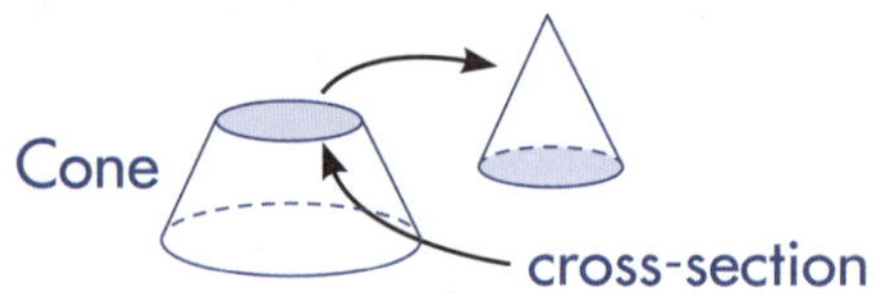

The cross-section of a cone is a circle.

A **top view** is what an object looks like when viewed from **above**.

We practise

Name this 3D object.

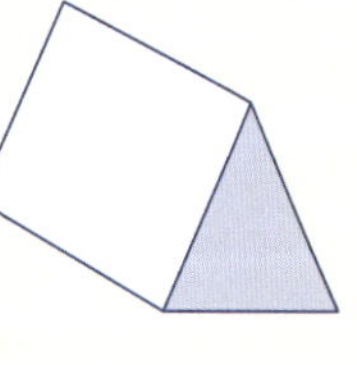

Triangular prism

If the following 3D object were sliced in half, what 2D shape would you see?

Circle

What 3D object will this net make?

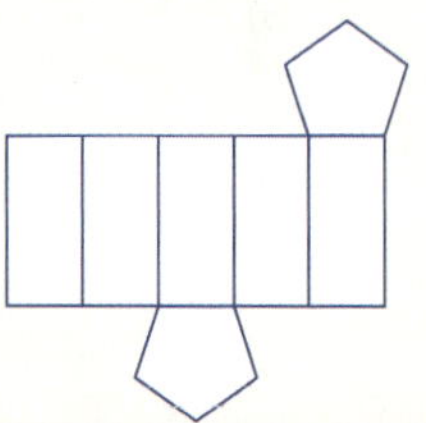

Pentagonal prism

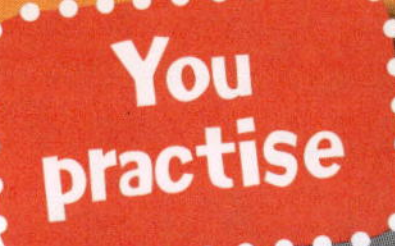

How many faces (F), edges (E) and vertices (V) does each 3D object have?

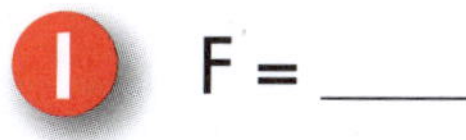

1 F = _____
E = _____
V = _____

2 F = _____
E = _____
V = _____

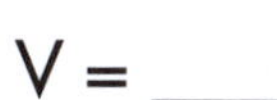

3 F = _____
E = _____
V = _____

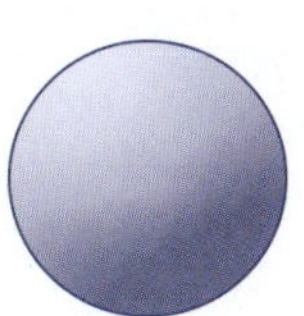

Name the 3D object you can make from each net.

4 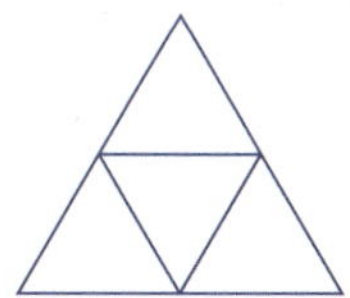

____

____

5 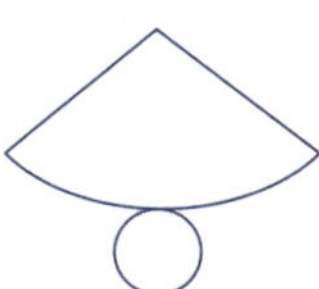

____

____

6 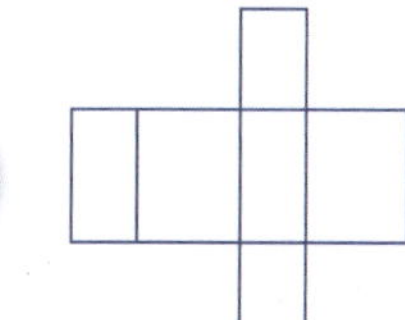

____

____

Draw lines to match each 3D object to its name.

7 Hexagonal prism

8 Hemisphere

9 Rectangular pyramid

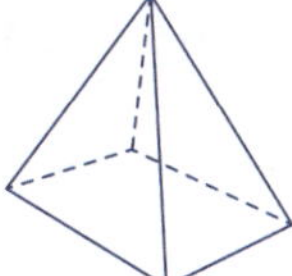

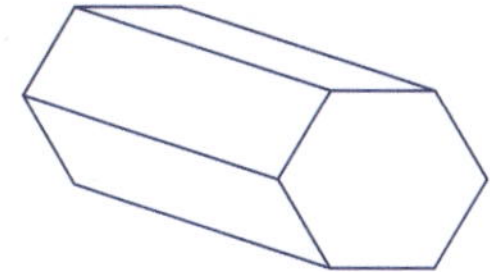

What 2D shapes are the cross-sections of these 3D objects?

10 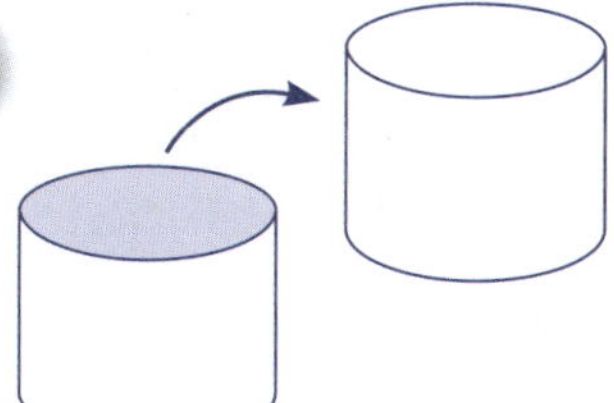

____

11 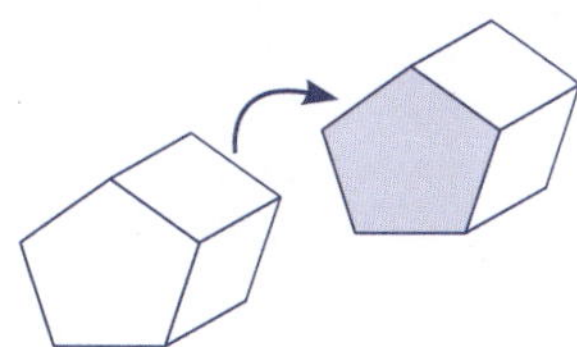

____

12 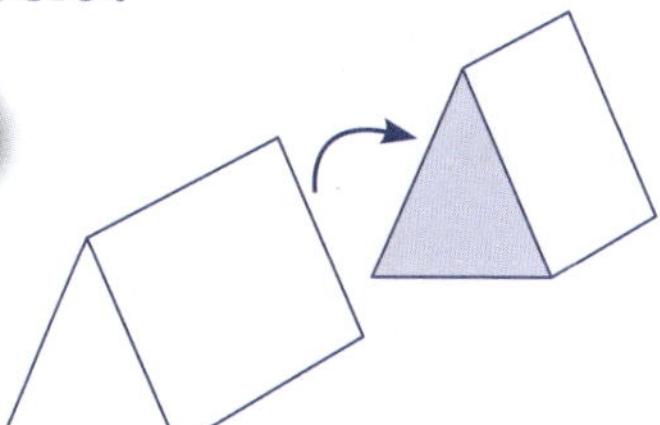

____

Problem solving

Two cones have been stuck together.
How many faces does this new object have?

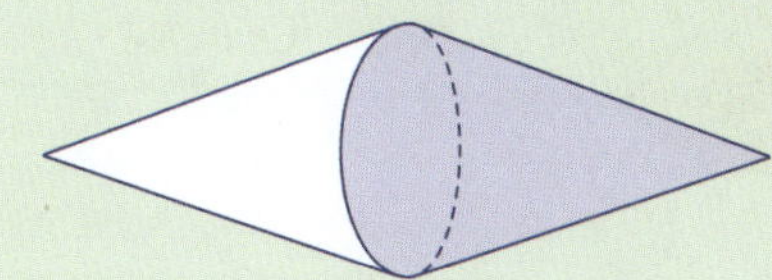

_____ faces

CHANCE

The **chance** of something happening tells us how likely it is to occur.
It is either **impossible** or **possible** that something can happen, but there is a range of possible outcomes.

Possible

Impossible — Very unlikely — Unlikely — Likely — Very likely or almost certain — Certain

These chance words are used to describe everyday events.

What are the chances of it raining today?
It is **likely** it will rain today.

What are the chances that school will be cancelled on Monday?
It is **very unlikely** that school will be cancelled on Monday.

What are the chances that you will eat some food today?
It is **very likely** or **almost certain** you will eat some food today.

Here are more chance words: probable, improbable, could, might, maybe, always, never, definite, uncertain, sure, 50:50.

Chance words can also describe the likelihood of you doing something.

What are the chances you will pick out a yellow lolly?
It is **likely** that you will pick out a yellow lolly.

What colour are you most unlikely to pull out?
You are most unlikely to pull out a blue lolly.

We practise

What is the chance of it hailing sausages today? Circle your answer.

Certain	Very unlikely
Likely	Possible
Impossible	Almost certain
Unlikely	Very likely

What colour is the spinner arrow least likely to land on?

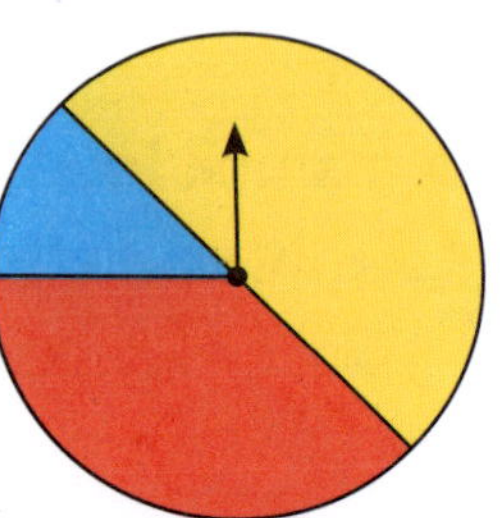

It is least likely to land on the blue colour.

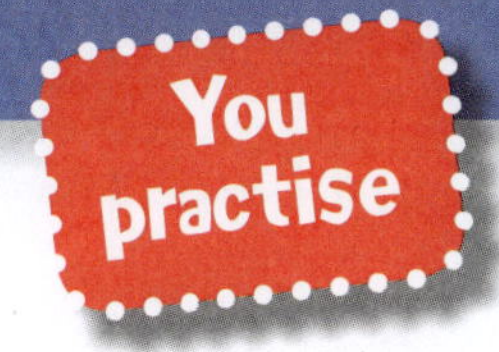

Draw a line from the everyday event to the chance word that describes it the best.

1	The Queen coming to visit you	Very likely
2	Your best friend turning into a frog	Likely
3	Eating something yummy today	Very unlikely
4	Going to sleep tonight	Certain
5	Flipping a coin and having it land on tails	Impossible

Look at the jar of marbles and answer these questions.
What are the chances that you will pick out:

6 a green marble? ____________________

7 a yellow marble? ____________________

8 a blue marble? ____________________

9 an orange marble? ____________________

Circle the answer that describes the event the best.
What are the chances you will spin and stop on:

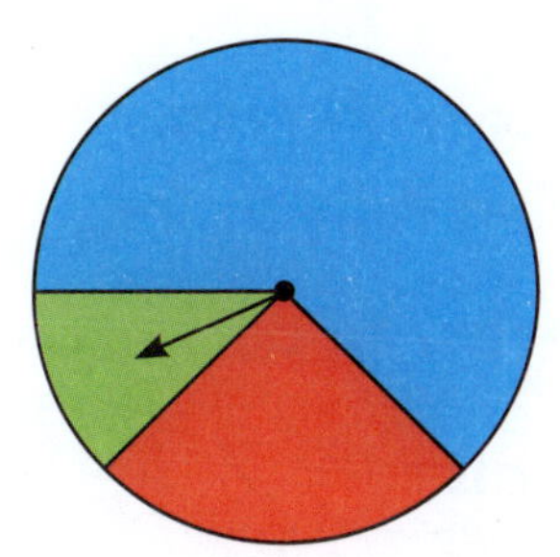

10	a blue colour?	Likely	Impossible
11	a green colour?	Likely	Unlikely
12	a red colour?	Likely	Almost certain

BOB time!

Problem solving

13 Jesse wanted to try his luck on the Lucky Dip at the school fair. He really wanted to get a teddy bear. What are his chances?

- ○ Likely
- ○ Impossible
- ○ Very unlikely
- ○ Certain

GRAPHS and DATA

Data is information that has been collected to answer a question about a topic. There are many ways this data can be represented to help answer the question.

Tally marks are quick markings to record how many times something happens or how much there is of something.

Tally marks are made in groups of 5 with the fifth mark going across.

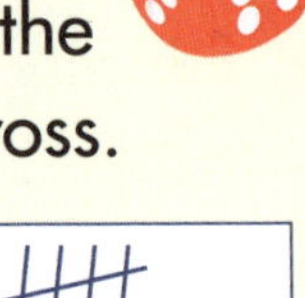

1	|||	4	~~||||~~
2	~~||||~~ |	5	~~||||~~ ||
3	||	6	||

The dice landed on the number four 5 times out of the 25 times it was rolled.

In column or bar graphs, information is recorded in vertical or horizontal columns.

The **title** describes what the graph is about.

A graph has a **vertical axis** and a **horizontal axis**.

Breakfast choices

Number of children: 0, 1, 2, 3, 4, 5, 6, 7

Toast, Pancakes, Cereal

Each axis either shows the **frequency** (how many) or what information is being gathered.

In picture graphs, pictures are used to represent 'how many' there are of something.

A picture graph is also called a **pictograph**.

Number of books read in Class 3P

We practise

Record the results using tally marks.

Favourite pets in Class 3R

Cats	7	~~||||~~ ||
Snakes	2	||
Dogs	5	~~||||~~

Use the above information to complete the column graph.

Favourite pets in Class 3R

Children playing sport after school

Year 1	⚽ ⚽
Year 2	⚽ ⚽ ⚽ ⚽
Year 3	⚽ ⚽ ⚽

Key: ⚽ = 5 children

How many children in Year 1 play sport after school?

10 children

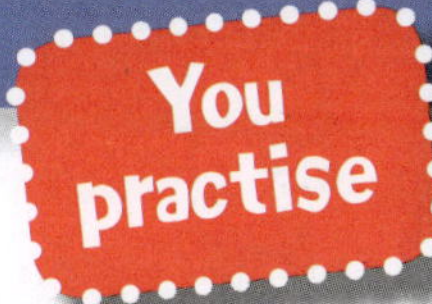

Use the tally marks to answer the following questions.

Favourite fruit	
Fruit	**Tally**
Watermelon	卌 |||
Oranges	卌	
Apples	卌 卌 |||

Transport to school	
Transport	**Tally**
Car	卌 卌	
Walk	卌 卌
Bus	|||

Favourite TV shows	
TV show	**Tally**
Deadly 60	卌
Funny Videos	卌 卌
Kids' News	||||

1. How many students said apples were their favourite fruit? ______

2. How many students travelled to school by car? ______

3. How many more students preferred Funny Videos to Kids' News? ______

Look at the graphs and answer the questions.

4. Which toy was the least popular? ____________

5. How many children liked Star Wars toys the best? ______

6. How many more children would need to like Monster High toys to make it the most popular? ______

7. How many children's favourite item of clothing was a jacket? ______

8. How many children liked shoes and hats altogether? ______

Problem solving

9. If Ned sold lemonade for $4.00 a glass, how much money did he make on Tuesday? ________

10. How much did he make altogether on Monday and Thursday? ________

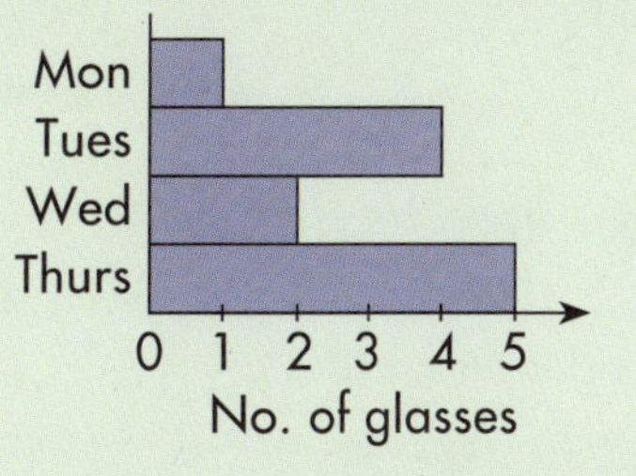

ANSWERS

Unit 1

1. 48
2. 50
3. 96
4. 158
5. 52
6. 20
7. 75
8. 117
9. 22 bookmarks
10. $36

Unit 2

1. 4 rows of 4, 4 × 4 = 16
2. 2 rows of 3, 2 × 3 = 6
3. 3 rows of 5, 5 × 3 = 15
4. 16
5. 6
6. 15
7. 30
8. 25
9. 28
10. 8
11. 4
12. 2
13. 6 × 4 = 24
14. 12 × 3 = 36
15. 8 × 5 = 40
16. 2 rows of 8 biscuits (2 × 8 = 16)
17. 4 biscuits each (16 ÷ 4 = 4)

Unit 3

1			4	3	7
2		5	8	2	1
3	8	5	3	4	8
4				1	4

5. Tens
6. Thousands
7. Ones
8. Ten thousands
9. 386 = 300 + 80 + 6
10. 97 105 = 90 000 + 7000 + 100 + 5
11. 4583 = 4000 + 500 + 80 + 3
12. 21 520 = 20 000 + 1000 + 500 + 20
13. Forty-five thousand, six hundred
14. Seven hundred and ninety-two
15. Take away 300

Unit 4

1. 20, 25, 30. Rule: + 5
2. 29, 31, 33. Rule: + 2
3. 50, 40, 30. Rule: – 10
4. 1008, 1012, 1016. Rule: + 2
5. 
6. 
7. 20, 30, 40, 50, 60, 70. Rule: + 10
8. 14, 16, 18, 20, 22, 24. Rule: + 2
9. 3, 6, 9

Unit 5

1. 62, 63, 69. Arrow = 63
2. 420, 480. Arrow = 465
3. 250 mL
4. 35 g
5. 65 mm
6. 3 L
7. 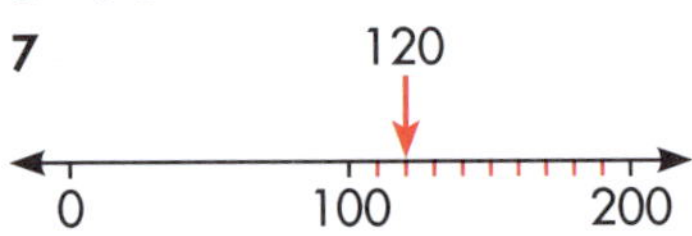

8. 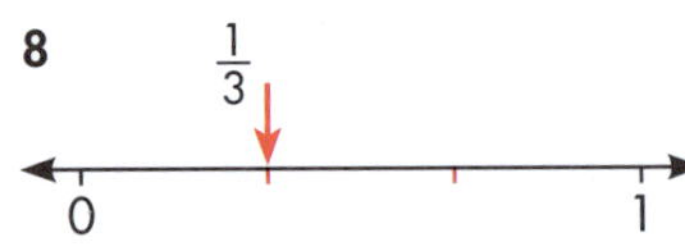

9. $\frac{3}{4}$ L

Unit 6

1. True
2. True
3. False
4. False
5. 4th
6. 6th
7. Blue
8. 5th
9. 97, 98, 99, 100, 101
10. 2, 906, 908, 2005, 2101
11. 527, 521, 418, 411, 401
12. 6745, 6645, 5745, 5645
13. 1st: Maya (98 sec), 2nd: Jack (102 sec), 3rd: Jo (112 sec), 4th: Zoe (114 sec), 5th: Otis (120 sec), 6th: Neri (133 sec)

Unit 7

1. $\frac{3}{4}$
2. $\frac{2}{3}$
3. $\frac{2}{2}$
4. 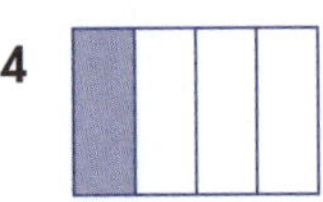
5. 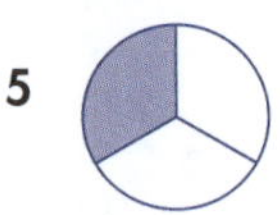
6. 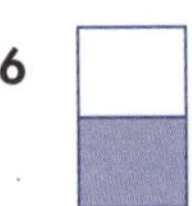
7. $1\frac{1}{2}$
8. $3\frac{1}{3}$
9. $\frac{3}{6}$ or $\frac{1}{2}$
10. $\frac{5}{8}$
11. 
12. 
13. 
14. 
15. $\frac{8}{12}$ 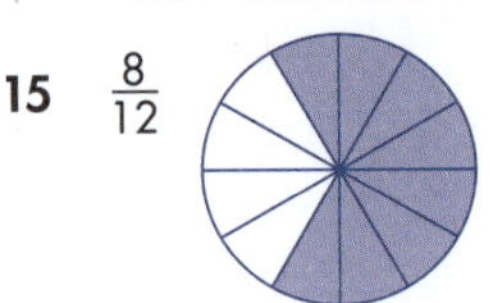

Unit 8

1. $\frac{2}{4}$
2. $\frac{4}{8}$
3. $\frac{2}{6}$
4. $\frac{2}{8}$
5. $\frac{2}{10}$
6. $\frac{4}{10}$
7. $\frac{6}{8}$

ANSWERS

8 $\frac{6}{6}$

9 $\frac{1}{3} = \frac{2}{6}$ cake

10 $\frac{3}{6} = \frac{1}{2}$ avocado

11 $\frac{2}{3} = \frac{4}{6}$ pizza

12 $\frac{6}{8} = \frac{3}{4}$ chocolate bar

13 $\frac{3}{4}$

Unit 9

1 $6.85
2 $5.20
3 $4.15
4 $5.40
5 Toby
6  
7   
8   
9 $3.45

Unit 10

1
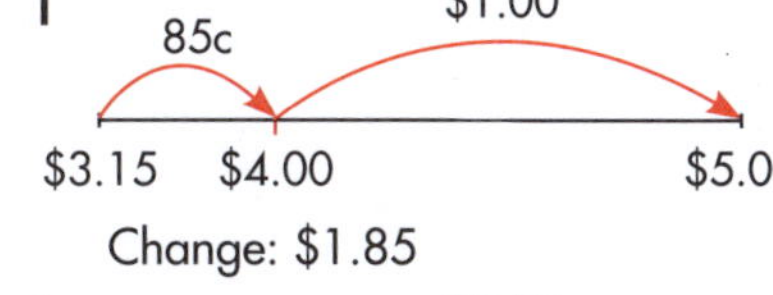

Change: $1.85

2
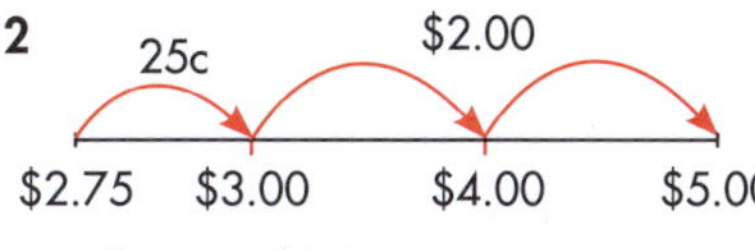

Change: $2.25

3
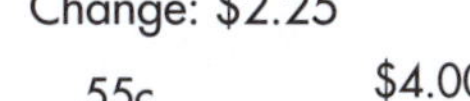

Change: $4.55

4

Change: $1.25

5 $1.40
6 $2.75
7 $3.55
8 $1.85
9 3 × 50c = $1.50
$5.00 – $1.50 = $3.50
Change = $3.50

Unit 11

1 12 cm
2 1.75 kg or 1 kg 750 g
3 1.1 L or 1 L 100 mL
4 1.8 m or 1 m 80 cm
5 4.59 m or 4 m 59 cm
6 56.82 m or 56 m 82 cm
7 5.69 kg or 5 kg 690 g
8 4200 mL or 4 L 200 mL
9 2930 m
10 25.2 cm or 25 cm 2 mm
11 9.266 km or 9 km 266 m
12 5710 g
13 9 cm
14 1.2 L

Unit 12

1 22 minutes past 10; 10:22
2 10 minutes past 3; 3:10
3 36 minutes past 5; 5:36
4 9 minutes to 8; 7:51
5 18 minutes to 4; 3:42
6 26 minutes to 9; 8:34
7 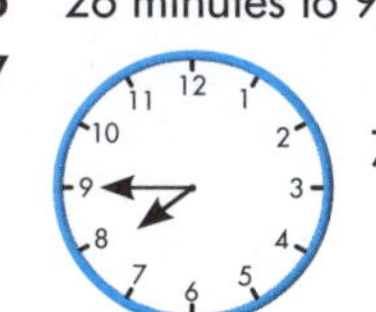 7:45
8 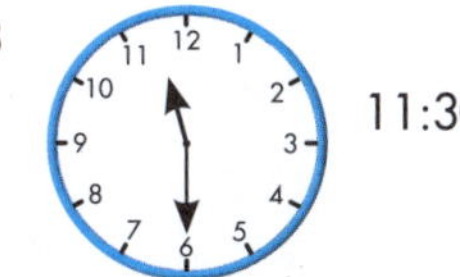 11:30
9  4:15
10 8:36

Unit 13

1 17th May
2 4
3 9th May
4 Monday
5 Thursday
6 2 h 30 min
7 9:00 am
8 4:00 am
9 Mia
10 Tim needs to leave home at 8:25 am.

Unit 14

1 F4
2 F2
3 B3
4 A1
5 C5 and D5
6 A6 and B6
7 A3
8 D2 and D3
9

	A	B	C	D	E	F	G
8		Z					W
7	S		O		Q		
6				C		O	
5		G					F
4	N			K		L	
3			B				
2	R				D		
1			O				M

GOOD WORK

10 C4

Unit 15

1 Pool
2 Year 3 classroom
3 Prep classroom
4 Tennis courts
5 Eating area
6 Cricket pitch
7 Go South three squares. Turn 90° clockwise and go straight ahead.

Unit 16

1 0 lines of symmetry
2 1 line of symmetry
3 2 lines of symmetry
4 3 lines of symmetry
5 4 lines of symmetry
6 6 lines of symmetry
7 
8 
9 

ANSWERS

10 

11

12 

13 3 sides; 3 lines of symmetry

14 4 sides; 4 lines of symmetry

15 5 sides; 5 lines of symmetry

16 6 sides; 6 lines of symmetry

17 Pattern: Each shape has the same number of sides as lines of symmetry.

18 The numerals 0, 3 and 8 are symmetrical.

Unit 17

1 Triangle

2 Square

3 Hexagon

4 Triangle (scalene)

5 Rectangle

6 Hexagon

7 

8

9 8 sides 

10 3 sides 

11 2 sides 

12 7 triangles

Unit 18

1 F = 3, E = 2, V = 0

2 F = 6, E = 12, V = 8

3 F = 1, E = 0, V = 0

4 Triangular pyramid

5 Cone

6 Rectangular prism

7 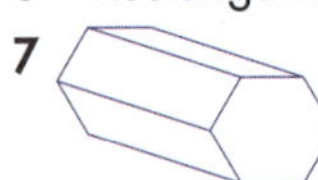 8 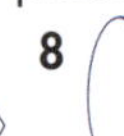 9 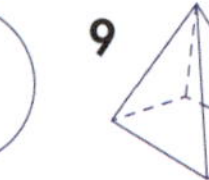

10 Circle 

11 Pentagon

12 Triangle

13 2 faces

Unit 19

1 Very unlikely

2 Impossible

3 Very Likely

4 Certain

5 Likely

6 Very likely

7 Very unlikely

8 Likely

9 Impossible

10 Likely

11 Unlikely

12 Likely

13 Very unlikely

Unit 20

1 13

2 11

3 6

4 Hot Wheels

5 8

6 5

7 6

8 12

9 Ned made $16.00 on Tuesday.

10 Altogether Ned made $24.00 on Monday and Thursday.

Sample NAPLAN test

1 46 – 30 = 16

2 100 cm

3 5 × 7

4 17 minutes to 11

5 73 643

6 14

7 140

8 B5

9 50 100

10  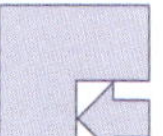

11 4th

12 8

13 

14

15 $\frac{1}{6}$

16 

17 $6.80

18 Very unlikely

19 $2.60

20 20

21 15 cm

22 1 L 700 mL

23 10 lollies

24 45 minutes past 7 and quarter to 8

25 Add 4000

26 8:00

27

28 G3, B1, F1

29 200 mL

30 Library

31 50 + 2

32

33 $\frac{9}{15}$

34

35 $\frac{4}{6}$

36 Rectangle

37 

38 Lemonade

39 $1.45

40 March had more rain than January.

Sample NAPLAN* test

Use 2B or HB pencil only. Time limit: 45 minutes.

Time started ___________ Time finished ___________

1 **46 – 16 = 30. Which number sentence is also true?**

- ○ 16 + 46 = 30
- ○ 30 – 16 = 46
- ○ 46 – 30 = 16
- ○ 30 – 46 = 16

2 **What is the height of the chair?**

○ 100 cm ○ 200 cm ○ 20 cm ○ 1.2 km

*This is not an officially endorsed publication of the NAPLAN program and is produced by Pascal Press independently of Australian Governments.

3 If 7 children each have 5 lollies, which problem best shows the way to find the total number of lollies?

- ○ 5 + 7
- ○ 5 × 7
- ○ 5 + 5 + 5 + 5
- ○ 7 − 5

4 What time did the school bell ring for morning tea?

- ○ 11 minutes past 9
- ○ 17 minutes to 10
- ○ 17 minutes to 11
- ○ 9 minutes past 11

5 70 000 + 3000 + 600 + 40 + 3 = ?

- ○ 76 343
- ○ 89 241
- ○ 73 643
- ○ 34 637

6 How many days are there in a fortnight?

- ○ 7
- ○ 15
- ○ 30
- ○ 14

7 Which number is missing in the number sequence?

110, 120, 130, _____ , 150, 160

- ○ 135
- ○ 170
- ○ 140
- ○ 100

8 If you were to move Table 4 up 3 squares, what would be its new coordinates?

Plan of 3F's classroom

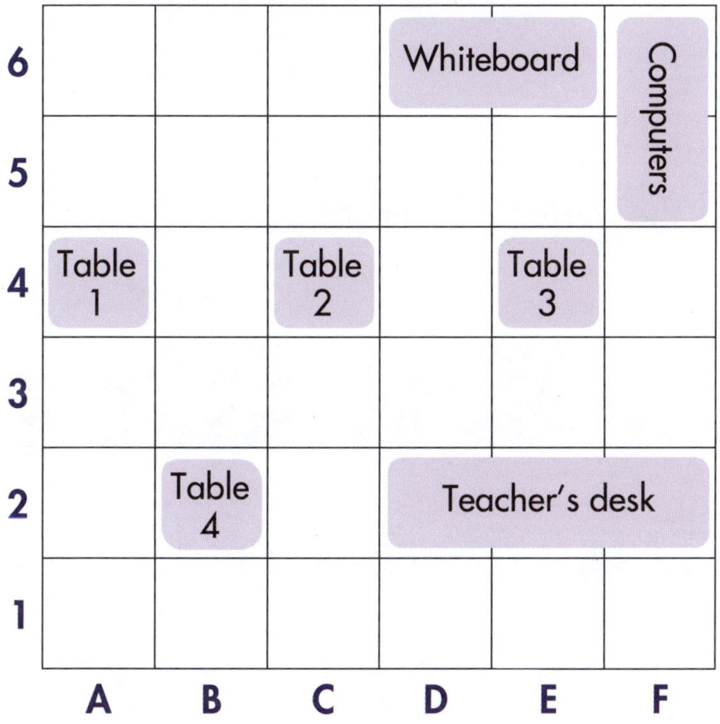

	A	B	C	D	E	F
6				Whiteboard	Whiteboard	Computers
5						Computers
4	Table 1		Table 2		Table 3	
3						
2		Table 4		Teacher's desk	Teacher's desk	Teacher's desk
1						

- ○ B2
- ○ 5C
- ○ B5
- ○ 5B

9 

Which arrow is pointing to 78?

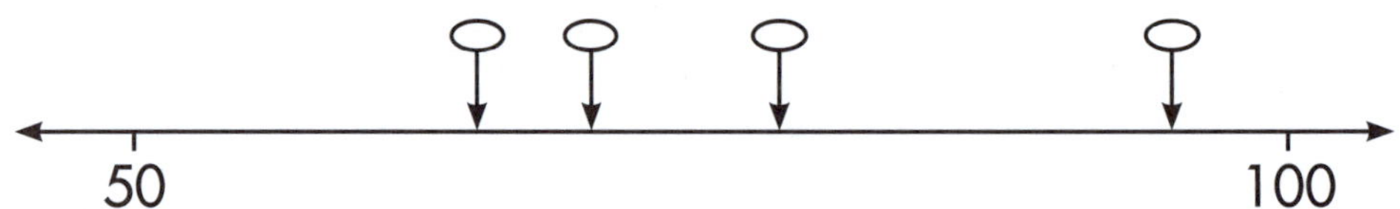

10 **What would this shape look like if you rotated it a three-quarter turn anticlockwise?**

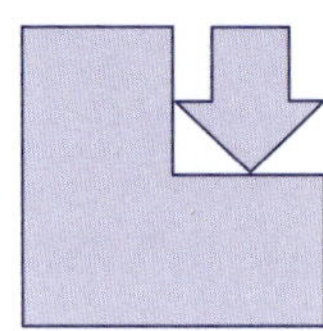

○ 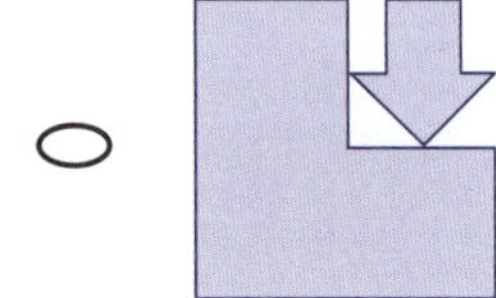

○ 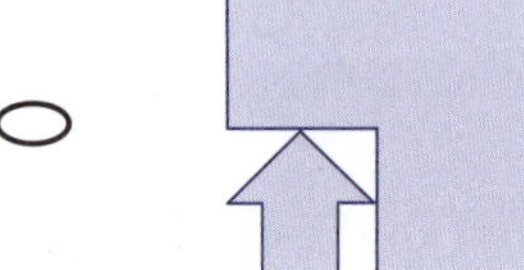

○ 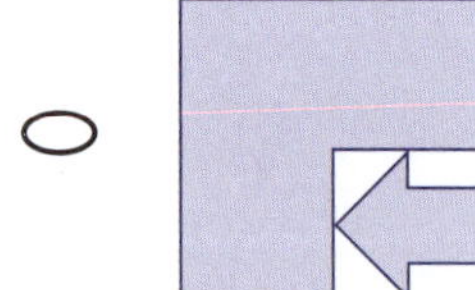

○ 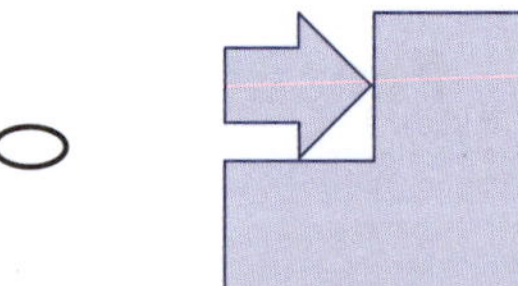

11 **What position is the motor scooter in?**

○ 1st ○ 4th ○ 5th ○ 3rd

12 How many sides does an octagon have?

- ○ 5
- ○ 6
- ○ 7
- ○ 8

13 A row of buildings on the riverside looked like this:

What would its reflection in the river look like?

○ 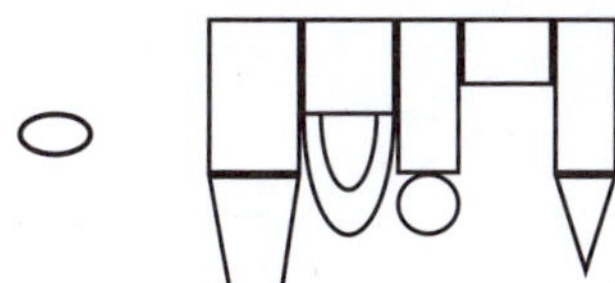

○ 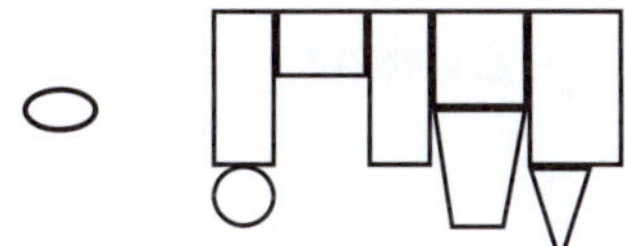

○ 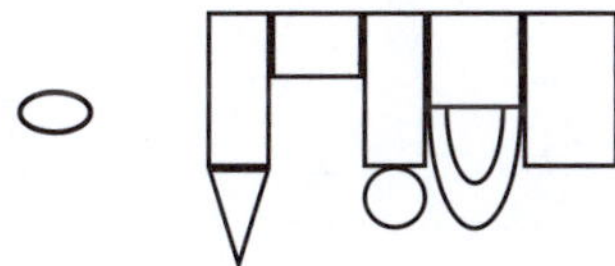

○ 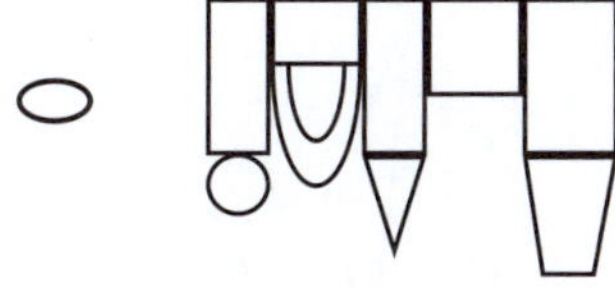

14 Which picture shows $\frac{3}{5}$?

○ 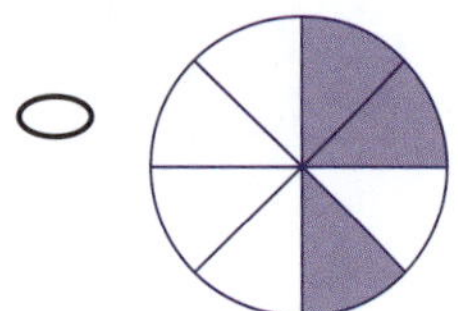

○

○

○

15 What is an equivalent fraction to $\frac{2}{12}$?

○ $\frac{1}{6}$ ○ $\frac{4}{8}$ ○ $\frac{2}{6}$ ○ $\frac{1}{12}$

16 Which of these shapes is a hexagonal pyramid?

○ 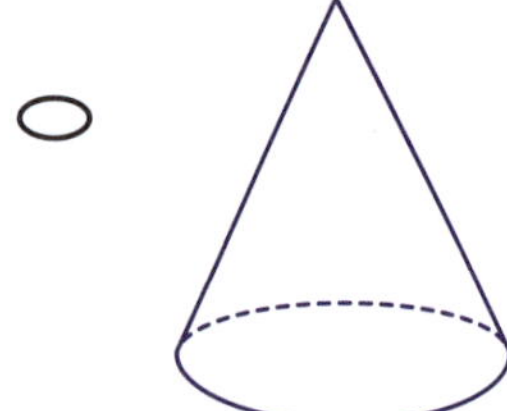

 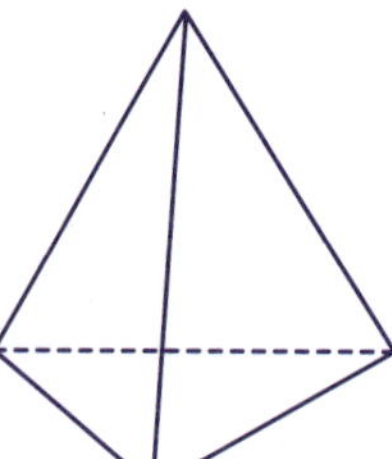

○ 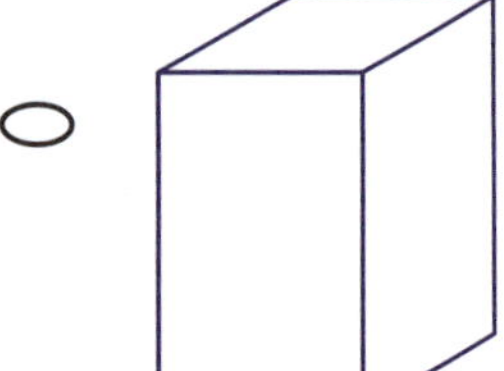

 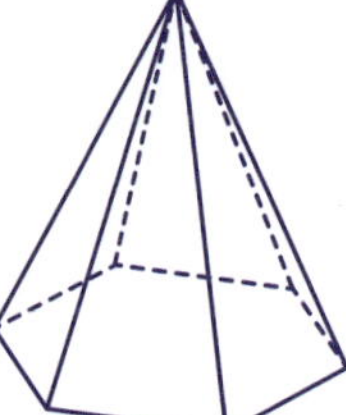

17 **Harrison has this much money to spend at the fair. How much does he have?**

- ○ $4.80
- ○ $6.60
- ○ $5.70
- ○ $6.80

---

18 **Peter rolled 2 dice to move ahead in a board game. What are the chances that he will roll 2 sixes?**

- ○ Impossible
- ○ Likely
- ○ Very unlikely
- ○ Certain

---

19 **If one marble costs $1.20, how much change will I get from $5.00 if I buy two marbles?**

- ○ $2.50
- ○ $2.60
- ○ 60c
- ○ $2.70

20 Altogether, how many Silver and Yellow cars passed the school?

Cars passing school	
Colour	**Tally**
Blue	卌
Yellow	卌 卌 I
Black	II
Silver	卌 IIII
White	卌 卌 卌
Red	卌 卌 II

- ○ 20
- ○ 19
- ○ 11
- ○ 13

21 Ben and Sam measured their height.
Ben was 126 cm and Sam was 111 cm.
How much did Sam have to grow to reach the height of Ben?

Bryony filled one drink bottle up with 500 mL of juice and another with 1.2 L of juice. How much juice did she have altogether?

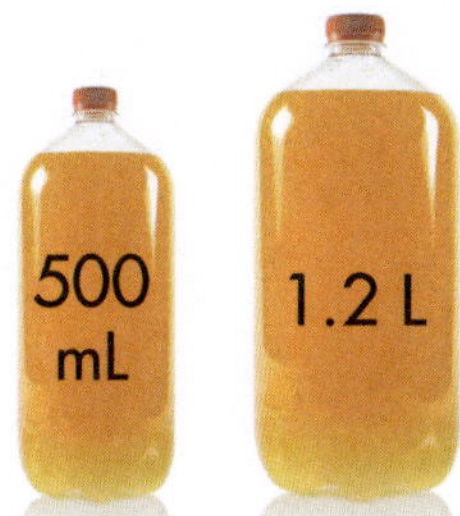

- ○ 612 L
- ○ 6.7 L
- ○ 1 L 700 mL
- ○ 1 L 520 mL

23 **Nadir had 40 lollies to put into party bags. If he put 5 lollies each in 6 party bags, how many lollies does he have left over?**

- ○ 20 lollies
- ○ 10 lollies
- ○ 35 lollies
- ○ 31 lollies

24 **What other ways can you write 7:45?**

- ○ 45 minutes past 7 and 15 minutes to 7
- ○ 15 minutes to 7 and quarter to 7
- ○ 15 minutes to 8 and quarter past 7
- ○ 45 minutes past 7 and quarter to 8

25 **Look at the two calculator displays. What did Joe have to do to change the first display into the second display?**

63 852	67 852

- ○ Minus 4000
- ○ Add 4000
- ○ Minus 400
- ○ Add 400

26 **What is the missing time on the timetable?**

Webster Road bus timetable				
Destination	**Time**			
Campbell Place	6:20	6:30	6:40	6:50
Main Street	7:50	?	8:10	8:20
High Street	9:00	9:10	9:20	9:30

- ○ 6:50
- ○ 7:50
- ○ 8:00
- ○ 8:30

27 What is the next shape in the following pattern?

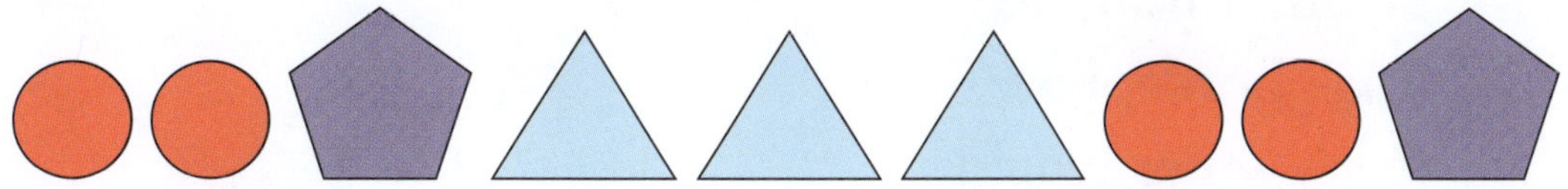

- ○ 
- ○ 
- ○ 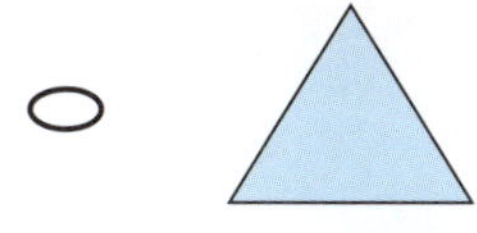
- ○ 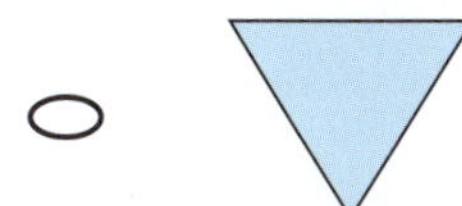

28 Leo spelt the word 'RAT' using coordinates.
What are they?

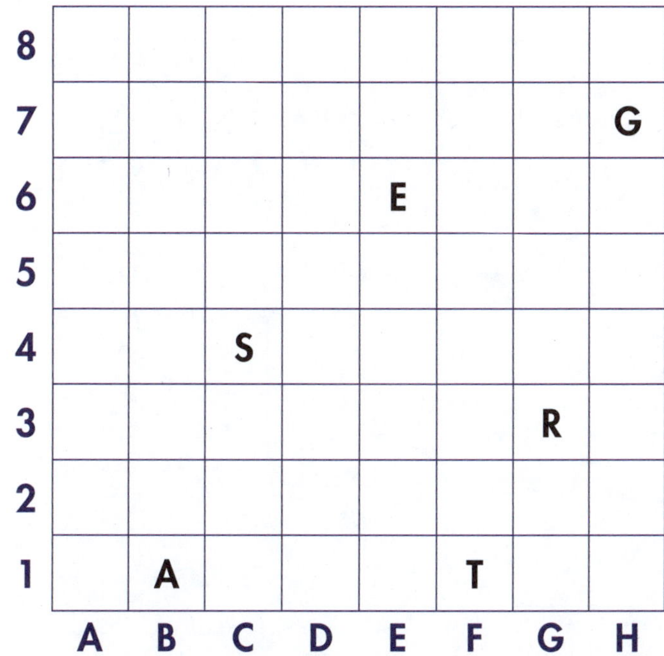

- ○ F1, GD, B1
- ○ G3, B1, F1
- ○ D6, B1, B5
- ○ G3, B0, B5

29 **If Alex drank 150 mL of water from his drink bottle, how much water would be left?**

- ○ 200 mL
- ○ 300 mL
- ○ 250 mL
- ○ 350 mL

30 **Oliver borrowed his friend's jet pack, which could make him fly in the air. If Oliver starts at the Kiosk and he flies directly East, what building will he land on?**

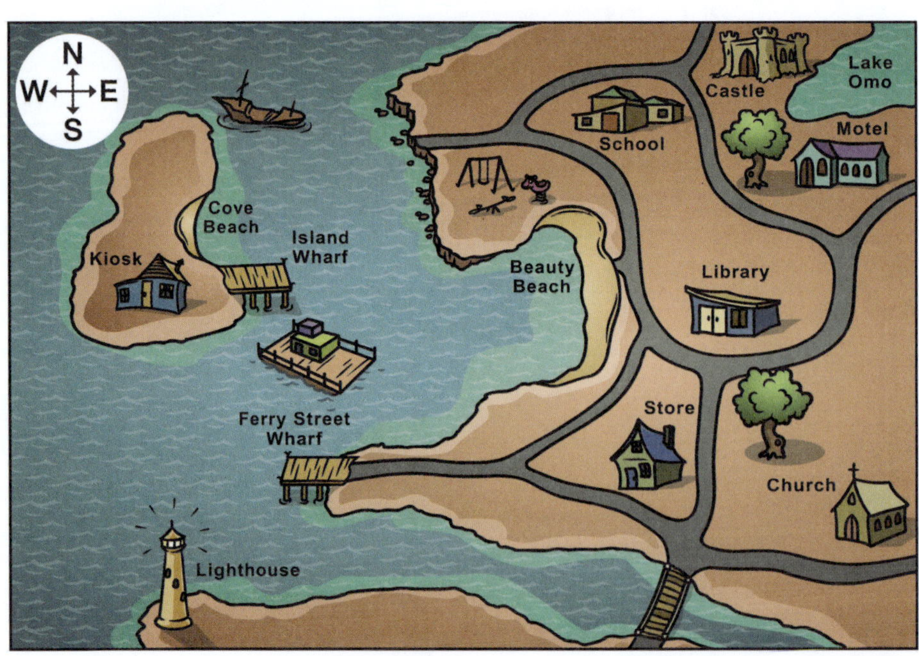

○ Store ○ Library ○ Church ○ School

31 Which of the following problems makes this statement true?

50 < □

○ 22 + 5 ○ 30 + 20 ○ 40 − 1 ○ 50 + 2

32 Which picture has more than two lines of symmetry?

○ 

○ 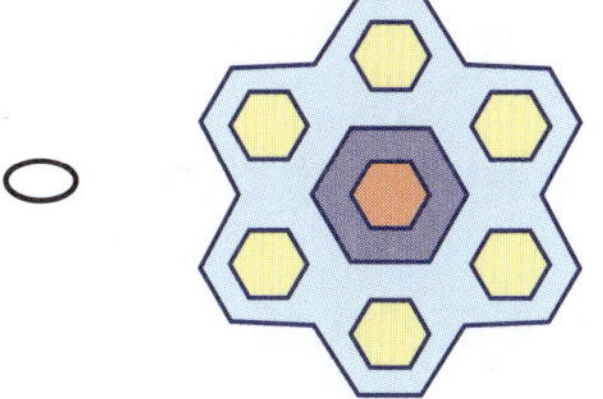

○ 

○ 

33 Jayden had 15 stickers in his pocket. He gave one each to 6 of his friends. What fraction of stickers did he have left?

○ $\frac{3}{4}$

○ $\frac{15}{6}$

○ $\frac{6}{15}$

○ $\frac{9}{15}$

34 
Which of the following shapes is a pentagon?

○ 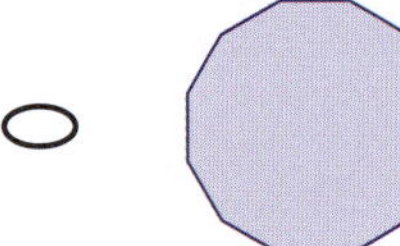

○ 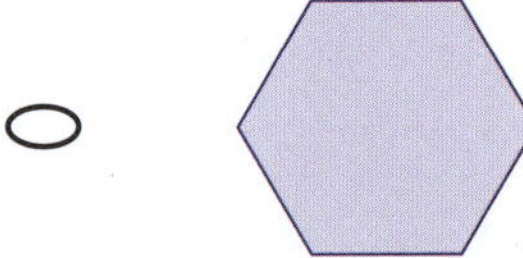

○ 

○ 

35 Isabel ate $\frac{2}{3}$ of a mince pie.

What fraction is equivalent to the amount she ate?

○ $\frac{3}{4}$

○ $\frac{4}{8}$

○ $\frac{4}{6}$

○ $\frac{1}{3}$

36 If the following 3D object were sliced in half, what 2D shape would be seen?

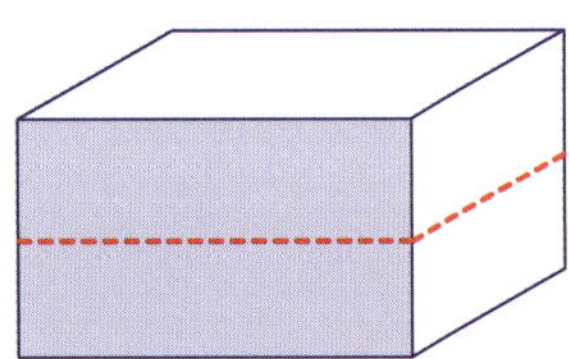

○ Square

○ Rectangular prism

○ Triangle

○ Rectangle

37 Which group of coins totals $2.75?

○ 

○ 

○ 

○ 

38 Liv bought a bag of ice creams to share with her friends. What flavour is the first person most likely to pull out?

Banana
Lime
Chocolate
Lemonade

○ Banana ○ Chocolate ○ Lemonade ○ Lime

39 Tony has these coins.

If Tony buys a belt for $7.10,
how much money will he have left over?

40 Which statement best describes this graph?

Weather conditions

January	
February	
March	

Key: = 5 days = 5 days

- ◯ January had more rainy days than February.
- ◯ March had 5 more sunny days than February.
- ◯ January and February combined had 15 days of rain.
- ◯ March had more rain than January.